SpringerBriefs in Economics

AF793695

More information about this series at http://www.springer.com/series/8876

John Komlos

Principles of Economics for a Post-Meltdown World

Springer

John Komlos
University of Munich
Munich
Germany

ISSN 2191-5504 ISSN 2191-5512 (electronic)
SpringerBriefs in Economics
ISBN 978-3-319-27827-8 ISBN 978-3-319-27828-5 (eBook)
DOI 10.1007/978-3-319-27828-5

Library of Congress Control Number: 2015959575

© The Author(s) 2016
This work is subject to copyright. All rights are reserved by the Publisher, whether the whole or part of the material is concerned, specifically the rights of translation, reprinting, reuse of illustrations, recitation, broadcasting, reproduction on microfilms or in any other physical way, and transmission or information storage and retrieval, electronic adaptation, computer software, or by similar or dissimilar methodology now known or hereafter developed.
The use of general descriptive names, registered names, trademarks, service marks, etc. in this publication does not imply, even in the absence of a specific statement, that such names are exempt from the relevant protective laws and regulations and therefore free for general use.
The publisher, the authors and the editors are safe to assume that the advice and information in this book are believed to be true and accurate at the date of publication. Neither the publisher nor the authors or the editors give a warranty, express or implied, with respect to the material contained herein or for any errors or omissions that may have been made.

Printed on acid-free paper

This Springer imprint is published by SpringerNature
The registered company is Springer International Publishing AG Switzerland

Preface

The goal of this volume is to demonstrate the ways in which introductory economics textbooks are deceptive, insofar as they insist on singing the praises of free markets, keeping any demurrals muted. I demonstrate this stealthy quality by "deconstructing" line-by-line the well-known textbook by Paul Samuelson and William Nordhaus, *Economics* (19th edition) (hereafter S&N). Note, however, that it is by no means the worst available. It is just one example among the many similarly flawed textbooks. The inconvenient truth is that current principles textbooks in use have changed very little, if at all, after the financial crisis, although their authors should have realized that their textbooks are inadequate for the post-Meltdown world. It is amazing that competition has not created a more appropriate outcome. No less an authority than Nobel Prize-winning economist Joseph Stiglitz declared prematurely after the crisis that "neoliberalism as a doctrine; market fundamentalism is dead."[1] Unfortunately, you would not know it by reading the textbooks in the field which influence millions of students, year in and year out.

Actually, the courses based on these textbooks are "toxic" for a number of reasons, including:

(a) They assume that people are rational, thereby completely disregarding the work of major contributors to the field such as Herbert Simon, Daniel Kahneman and Amos Tversky; in an important sense, the standard

[1]In a speech in November 2008, Stiglitz declared, "This September has been to market fundamentalism what the fall of the Berlin Wall was to communism. We all knew that those ideas were flawed, that free market ideology didn't work; we all knew that communism didn't work, but these were defining moments that made it clear that it didn't work. . . . America really has a system. . . . a kind of corporatism corporate welfareism. . . . under the guise of free market economics. And it is that mixture that was fundamentally flawed, incoherent, was intellectually bankrupt from the beginning, that has been shown not to work." Joseph Stiglitz—"Market Fundamentalism is Dead," YouTube video, posted by ForaTV, November 10, 2008. https://www.youtube.com/watch?v=x_2-Tv2GPs0, accessed, February 6, 2010.

assumptions in economics are anachronistic insofar as they are pre-Freudian and pre-Pavlovian.

(b) They disregard the effects of incomplete and asymmetric information on choice and on allocation of resources by overlooking the path-breaking work of scholars such as George Ackerlof and Joseph Stiglitz.

(c) They assume that tastes are exogenous—that is to say that people enter the economy with tastes fully formed—which, of course, is very far from reality. This is most important, because conventional economists do not consider feedback effects from the business community to influence individual tastes. Once that assumption is made, however, it is no longer possible to discuss the extent to which consumers are manipulated through Pavlovian conditioning, through the influence of the unconscious mind, and through cognitive capture. This is probably the most pernicious of the various assumptions.

(d) The default model in mainstream economics is the perfectly competitive model which is of negligible importance in today's world. Instead, oligopoly and monopolistic competition should be the default model. (The fact that S&N's textbook is selling currently for an exorbitant price of $307, although the cost of production of a volume is probably in the $15 range is a good example of oligopolistic pricing in such captive markets. After all, the students are compelled to purchase the textbook once it is assigned by the professor and the professor has no incentive to shop around for less expensive alternatives, although they do exist.[2]) Clinging on to the perfectly competitive model is a damaging strategy, because it enables policy makers to apply incorrect models to important issues of the day such as financial deregulation. In fact, this is the model that Alan Greenspan had in mind while he was in charge of the financial sector and why he ruled out the possibility of a destructive bubble. After all, bubbles do not occur in a perfectly competitive model with rational agents and perfect information. The damage to the world of his dogmatic insistence on mainstream orthodoxy should be obvious to everyone.

(e) Conventional economics textbooks overlook interdependencies. Yet, there are all sorts of externalities not only in production but in consumption as well. Hence, they overlook conspicuous consumption and its corollary: "keeping up with the Joneses," the quest for social status that often drives people into a debt trap from which they are unable to escape.

(f) Textbooks invariably provide examples of simple choice between two goods disregarding the challenges of more complex decisions in which quality and other intangible attributes are difficult—and often impossible—to ascertain. In addition, they neglect the fact that choice almost always involves a sequence of decisions which is computationally much more demanding than the no-brainers they offer as examples. In other words, the textbooks overlook the

[2]For example: Neva Goodwin, Jonathan M. Harris, Julie A. Nelson, Brian Roach, Mariano Torras, *Principles of Economics in Context*, (Routledge: 2014) is selling for $82.

fact that obtaining reliable information and path-dependence are two major hindrances to optimization.

(g) They pretend to be scientific and value free but end up being ideological through the assumptions they make. For example, the refusal to distinguish between basic needs and other goods leaves an ethical void in their teachings that enables them to take a neutral stance regarding price gauging in the pharmaceutical markets.

These examples are not exhaustive by any means. There are many other crucial concepts that are neglected in mainstream textbooks such as the important role of power, of transaction costs, and of uncertainty in determining economic outcomes. The above list merely illustrates some of the ways in which mainstream principles of economics textbooks distort our worldview with immense political, cultural, and economic consequences, as the financial crisis of 2008 demonstrated. However, students of economics deserve and need a more complete perspective and a more truthful rendering of the real-existing economy.

Thus, my goal in this volume is to critique the worldview of conventional economics and provide alternative perspectives. My version of free-market economics emphasizes that the human element should be paramount and moral judgments should override market outcomes to the extent these are not to the benefit of the common weal or distribute the benefits of economic activity disproportionally. In other words, what is important to me is not GNP as much as the quality of life; I believe that the focus should not be on inanimate objects or on abstract concepts but how people live and fare in the economy.

To be sure, many professors argue that introductory textbooks have to present a watered-down version of reality, because one has to lay the foundations before students can learn more sophisticated aspects of the discipline. In other words, principles textbooks should convey a very simple overview without getting bogged down in the details of more advanced ideas. Such justification for half-truths is, in my opinion, selling the readers way too short, is counterproductive, and is hardly warranted because the simplification distorts to such an extent that the students leave the course with a distorting caricature of the economy.

I think that a more realistic version is compulsory from the very beginning for at least four crucial reasons: (1) Half-truths do not belong in a scholarly publication, and especially not pretending to be the whole Truth and nothing but the Truth; (2) it is much easier to learn a discipline correctly the first time around than learn the watered-down version and have to unlearn it subsequently, as it is extremely difficult to unlearn something. The human mind is not that flexible once the neural networks are connected, they are hard to rewire; (3) the more sophisticated ideas are actually not so complicated and can be presented at the introductory level; (4) most of the more than a million annual readers of principles textbooks do not continue learning economics so they never do get the more sophisticated version of the discipline anyway and are therefore misled for the rest of their lives. Thereafter, these students, however, go on to become voters responsible for choosing among policies and newspaper editors or small-town mayors—in other words, their careers take them to responsible positions within the society—mistakenly thinking that they have understood the basics of markets and continue to believe that they work efficiently as a matter of course. Hence, it is most important to approach the first course in economics with a fuller perspective before one is socialized into thinking that competitive markets can always and everywhere provide efficient solutions automatically. Paraphrasing Frank Sinatra, half a Truth does not appeal to me.

While agreeing that markets are important and useful institutions I believe that we should control markets and not the other way around. Markets should be regulated so as to provide for the common good. I advocate Capitalism with a Human Face in the tradition of economists such as Joseph Stiglitz, John Kenneth Galbraith, and Robert Reich. I believe that creating a just economy should be on our agenda and that the fruits of such an economy would benefit all and not only a handful. In my just economy people would not be excluded from the labor market.

In contrast, in mainstream classrooms free markets become God's gift to humanity, government is the boogeyman, and taxation is a burden on society's well-being. But such claims are bogus! Taxes are used to finance schools, basic research, and infrastructure and markets go haywire without adequate government backstop as the recent "mother of all financial crises" so amply demonstrated. But most teachers of Econ 101 are immune to such evidence. After all, the models work perfectly well on the blackboard!

But the models are so simplistic that they present a caricature of the real existing economy. Charles Ferguson in his Oscar-winning documentary "*Inside Job*" demonstrated most vividly the culpability of academic economists. Stiglitz has also repeatedly warned that the invisible hand metaphor ought not be taken seriously: "the reason the invisible hand often seemed invisible was that it was not there. . . . Markets by themselves do not lead to economic efficiency. If we look at examples of market successes and failures around the world, we see that many are understandable in terms of economic theories based on imperfect markets in which governments must play an important role. . . ."[3] The Federal Reserve in Washington, DC had no less than 300 PhD economists working for it, yet were incapable of seeing the crisis brewing for years. Presumably those who dared to disagree with Greenspan's ideology that bubbles were nothing to worry about and that markets worked perfectly well without government supervision became outcasts.

So it should not be surprising that students around the world demand a more colorful palate of perspectives. After all, markets are man-made institutions. So the human element with its emotions and complex psychology should be an integral part of the discipline. These students do not want economics to become a branch of mathematics. There is a growing global resistance to the fantasy world created in mainstream courses. The walkout of students from their Principles of Economics class at Harvard in solidarity with the 'Occupy" movement is just one example of

[3]"Joseph Stiglitz: Smith's 'invisible Hand' a Myth?" YouTube video, posted by ForaTV, March 8, 2010. https://www.youtube.com/watch?v=9qjvwQrZmpk accessed June 1, 2014.

this realization.[4] They realized that the economics they were being taught was doctrinaire, failed to provide a balanced perspective on the real existing economy, and did not show sufficient empathy for the 45 million people living in poverty. No wonder, the economics being taught on blackboards in most classrooms makes it appear as though markets descended straight from heaven while maintaining a conspiracy of silence on the Achilles heals of free markets such as not paying sufficient attention to safety, not caring enough about the environment, accepting an obscene distribution of income and wealth, and being indifferent to the welfare of future generations.

A group of students in 16 countries are also pushing back on the arrogance of mainstream economists and are demanding that a more realistic economics be taught with fewer abstractions, less emphasis on mathematical methods of problem solving, and more attention devoted to the plight of the real-world economies.[5] They are resisting the mainstream's view that super rationality reigns in the market inhabited by consumers with sufficient brain power to know every detail of the economy and therefore are not satisfied with anything less than achieving an optimum outcome. They do not believe that most people possess perfect understanding of all the nuances in small print and perfect foresight from the beginning to the end of their lives and are not inhibited by the challenges of information overload insofar as information is not free, not available instantaneously, and not a cinch to understand.

To be sure, markets do work perfectly well on the blackboard. However, what the students are demanding is that they work as well in real life and not only in Fairfax County, VA—one of the higher income counties in the USA—but also in the South Bronx, NY, a low-income slum. In other words, they are demanding a paradigm switch in the curriculum of Econ 101. This volume is a step in that direction. It should make it possible for students to understand the weaknesses of the mainstream approach and for professors to offer alternative perspectives.

---

[4]Jose A. Delreal, "Students Walk Out of Ec10 in Solidarity with 'Occupy'," *The Harvard Crimson*, November 2, 2011, http://www.thecrimson.com/article/2011/11/2/mankiw-walkout-economics-10/, accessed July 22, 2014.

[5]John Cassidy, "Rebellious Economics Students Have a Point," *The New Yorker*, May 13, 2014. http://www.newyorker.com/online/blogs/johncassidy/2014/05/rebellious-economics-students-have-a-point.html, accessed November 21, 2014.

Contents

Contents

Chapter 1
Basic Concepts

"Ours is a world of scarcity… A situation of scarcity is one in which goods are limited relative to desires." "Given unlimited wants…" (S&N p. 4). These assertions are influenced by the culture of the authors and certainly not one of the "truths" of economics that they claim to represent. Actually, these are assumptions insofar as no empirical evidence is presented in their support. You would not think that there was a scarcity of goods if you looked at our department stores or parking lots of auto dealerships. Note, also that they pertain to two variables: available goods and desires. Furthermore, our desires are not endless and depend crucially on external influences.

The most fundamental problem of the free-market system is that we are not at all allowed to develop our own desires without massive interference from the business community. Instead, the free market gives large corporations the opportunity to devote immense sums of money to manipulate us in order to influence our desires. This process of socialization begins at a very early age. Madison Avenue spends $300 billion urging us to spend our money today rather than tomorrow, because tomorrow the discounts will not be available any longer.[1] That is about as much as spent on automobiles or on gasoline in the USA annually.[2] However, advertisements urging us to be frugal and save for a rainy day are nonexistent. That is not in the interest of the corporate community. Thus, Madison Avenue increases our desires to own stuff well beyond our natural inclinations.[3]

What is worse, most people are unaware of this interference in their natural freedom to retain their identity without outside interference, i.e., this psychological infringement into their inner self. Through advertisement campaigns we are slowly and incrementally manipulated by the system without consciously realizing it and

[1]Wikipedia contributors, "Advertising" http://en.wikipedia.org/wiki/Advertising accessed October 9, 2014.
[2]Bureau of Economic Analysis, US Department of Commerce. November 23, 2010, Table 3. Gross Domestic Product and Related Measures: Level and Change from Preceding Period.
[3]Peter Whybrow, *American Mania, When More is not Enough* (New York: W.W. Norton, 2005).

© The Author(s) 2016

J. Komlos, *Principles of Economics for a Post-Meltdown World*,
SpringerBriefs in Economics, DOI 10.1007/978-3-319-27828-5_1

knowing the extent to which our will power and attitudes have been influenced. We become acculturated into an extreme form of consumerism and instant gratification spreads through the culture like an epidemic. The power and wealth of corporations is leveraged into an immense infringement on our freedoms. The more freedom there is in the marketplace, the less free are consumers on account of the fact that they have less power than the corporations. That is how we have gotten to be as indebted and as overweight as we are. And of course, being in debt is itself constricting, i.e., it limits our freedom. It is an immense cultural contradiction that a nation that values freedom most of all, as Americans do, evolves into an indebted nation, which, in turn, limits the freedom of the population immensely. This is one of the important reasons why the free market as now construed is unable to lead to satisfactory lives in half the population. Yet, S&N keep utterly silent about the immense businesses influence on our desires.

As a matter of fact, most of our desires, except the obvious basic needs,—including food, clothing, shelter, and health services—are culturally determined. They are not fixed at birth and are by no means natural: babies are not born with a desire for iphones. Hence, one should consider where our desires come from. S&N completely ignore this crucial issue throughout the text.

And what do they mean "given unlimited wants"? Given by who? What they mean is that they will assume that wants are unlimited, but they are not. Rather, Madison Avenue continually manipulates our wants. We are not as greedy as S&N imply. They also fail to distinguish between the reasons for wanting something. Surely, there is a fundamental difference between need for food and the desire to own a trendy cell phone. One is associated with human nature and survival, while the other is a need learned and acquired from the society in which we live. Moreover, in the affluent industrial societies the basic needs of the necessities of life is only about half of our total expenditures. There is only so much food, clothing, shelter, and health services we can consume.

"An economy is producing efficiently when no individual's economic welfare can be improved unless someone else is made worse off" (S&N p. 4). This definition is more controversial than it seems on first sight, because it implicitly accepts the current distribution of income as sacrosanct and efficient. This is hardly warranted as the current distribution of income is neither just nor the most productive possible. How can it be efficient if it is not lead to the most productive economy? For instance, many very productive persons may well have no capital to start a business and no collateral to gain access to capital although they would efficient producers if given the opportunity. Many children do not have access to decent schools and therefore are not going to be efficient producers as adults, but this definition does not allow us to redistribute income from the rich to the poor school districts so that the poor can also have decent schools. The current distribution may also not be ethical. Consider the system of slavery. Under the above definition, it was efficient because emancipation would have made the slave owners worse off.

This definition of efficiency is never invoked in macroeconomics because practically no policy action could be undertaken from this perspective insofar as all economic policy invariably makes some people worse off without being compensated for their losses. For instance, most economists and policy makers argued and continue to argue that the creation of NAFTA (the North American Free Trade Agreement) made Americans better off on average by improving economic efficiency. Yet, many people were hurt by it. Hence, from the point of view of the above definition it would not have been efficient to adopt the new policy. There are many inconsistencies between the micro- and the macroeconomic sections of their textbook.

The same is true for technological change: It is also never efficient according to the above definition as it never benefits everyone. Some people invariably find themselves at a disadvantage in the wake of an innovation.[4] The only time the definition is really invoked is when it comes to a redistributive policy. Then, economists argue forcefully against redistribution on the basis of the above definition but never do so when it comes to innovation, technological change, or international trade agreements. A rule that requires that an alternative allocation leave no participant worse off overwhelmingly favors the status quo and therefore protects the privileges of the wealthy and tilts the playing field against the poor and underprivileged. It is therefore not useful in policy applications.

I would propose an alternative definition of efficiency: "An economy is producing efficiently if a reallocation of resources could not increase output." The current economic system would not be considered efficient then. The total educational achievement and future productivity of the next generation could be increased substantially by equalizing the resources available to the youth of this country. In other words, a transfer of funds from the conspicuous consumption of the wealthy to poor school systems in order to bring them up to par would increase the productivity and hence the future efficiency of the economy in the next generation without emptying the pocketbooks of the wealthy. Hence, redistribution can be approached also from a perspective of efficiency not only from the perspective of fairness.

Stressing efficiency throughout the text is also a function of their cultural attitudes. It is not universally so important to all scholars. Many are more interested in a fair system in which the fruits of the economy are distributed in a fair and equitable fashion. That, however, is not high on their agenda.

"Economists use the scientific approach" (S&N p. 5). Economics is not at all like a science, because it is based on assumptions many of which are grounded in ideology. Alternative theories as well as facts from other disciplines are disregarded which scientists are normally not allowed to do. Would chemists be allowed to disregard results from physics or physics from mathematics? Certainly not! Yet, economists think that they can disregard scholarship from psychology, political science, or sociology. That cannot be the basis of a scientific approach. Social psychology, for example, frames the problem of human action in terms of group

[4]Some argue that hypothetical compensation should suffice for efficiency. According to this theory compensation does not actually have to take place, but mere possibility of compensation suffices. Thus, as long as gainers gain more than losers lose, the policy is efficient, but of course the theoretical possibility of compensation does not help the lives of those who lose and is therefore not a humanistic approach to economic policy as losers are never compensated by the winners. Leaving some people worse off is cruel economic policy.

dynamics. However, such group interactions are disregarded, in the main, by economists, although economic activity obviously does take place in a society and not between isolated individuals. We do not live like Robinson Crusoe. Yet, economists continue to rely on methodological individualism although it makes little sense in the complex society in which we live.

Furthermore, economists are much more limited in the ways in which they can run controlled experiments than are natural scientists. In simplifying people's behavior and motivation, they reduce them to robots but, of course, people are complex psychological creatures and do not conform to economists' simplifications. As a consequence, the predictions of basic economic theory have not been very reliable. Greenspan's interpretation of economic theory claimed that deregulation will improve the efficiency of markets and furthermore that markets will not crash. Yet, deregulation had just the opposite effect: Instead of improving efficiency, it led to a major financial crisis. Yet, economists are in no a hurry to revise their lecture notes and textbooks based on this empirical evidence. In other words, theory trumps empirical observation which leads to an immense insensitivity to evidence that contradicts the basic assumptions of economic discipline. Falsifiability is an important aspect of any scientific research program, but economic theory seems not to be falsifiable in the view of most of its mainstream practitioners and is therefore closer to a doctrine than to a science. Hence, S&N's approach is pseudo-scientific.

"We must carefully distinguish questions of fact from questions of fairness. Positive economics describes the facts of an economy, while normative economics involves value judgments" (S&N p. 6). This is an artificial distinction, because what one considers positive economics is itself a value judgment. S&N would consider their assumption that wants are unlimited positive economics whereas I consider it merely a part of their ideology. Their definition of efficiency is arbitrary. As far as they are concerned, the great increase in income is indicative of great progress, but they overlook unabashedly the concomitant social problems and the dizzying increase in inequality.

"Positive economics deals with questions such as: Why do doctors earn more than janitors?" (S&N p. 6). But their version of positive economics is superficial because they do not discuss the role of the American Medical Association in restricting the number of students of medicine, thereby inflating doctors' salaries to ridiculous levels. American doctors earn five times as much as Japanese doctors. I doubt seriously that they are five times more productive as well. Only half of those applying to medical schools are accepted, yet there is a shortage of general practitioners. The shortage of doctors will reach 90,000 by 2020 yet the medical profession is fighting foreign medical schools sending their students to the USA to do their residency.[5]

[5]Anemona Hartocollis, "Medical Schools in Region Fight Caribbean Flow," *The New York Times*, December 22, 2010. http://www.nytimes.com/2010/12/23/nyregion/23caribbean.html?_r=1&hp accessed October 9, 2014.

"Society must try to combine the discipline of the marketplace with the compassion of social programs" (S&N p. 7). It seems rather uncanny to talk about the discipline of the marketplace at a time when some of the biggest firms in the economy are protected from their mistakes by current and future taxpayers as represented by the Treasury Department and by the Federal Reserve. Their book was published in 2009 after the bailouts were under way. While Everyman on Main Street does have to face the discipline of the marketplace, the financiers of Wall Street continue to enjoy the privileges and their bonuses provided by the federal bailouts, guarantees, and subsidies.[6] The CEOs of Goldman Sachs and J.P. Morgan Chase were able to collect their $10 million salaries, while their banks and the whole financial system were propped up by Uncle Sam. To date, some $7 trillion worth of support of one sort or another has been put on the table for the Lords of Wall Street. Joseph Stiglitz calls these developments "ersatz capitalism" (phony capitalism) or "socialism for the rich and capitalism for the poor." Moreover, big business also evaded the discipline of the marketplace through their massive lobbying efforts. They have obtained subsidies, earmarks, and government contracts. The discipline was retained for Everyman on Main Street many of whom were evicted even though the banks did not even take the trouble of doing it legitimately and in their haste used illegal "robosigning" procedures as a shortcut to facilitate the evictions. It is amazing that they got away with it.

"Every society must have a way of determining what commodities are produced, how these goods are made, and for whom they are produced" (S&N p. 7). S&N simplify excessively by reducing the economic problem to these three aspects. We also need to determine the institutions that will regulate the economy and provide enforcement mechanisms for those regulations. What rules govern markets, property rights, and taxes? We also need to make contingency plans to take care of the unemployed and for those who are unable to meet their basic needs. Do we allow trusts, monopolies, oligopolies, or insider trading? How powerful do we allow corporations to be? How much outsourcing will be allowed? Taxation is an important issue because that will determine how much money will be allocated to public goods such as schools, roads, and basic research. These issues are crucial because those institutions will influence the allocation of production profoundly.

We also need institutions to protect the health and safety of consumers as well as the environment, minimize pollution, and preserve natural resources and ecosystems for subsequent generations.[7] These are by no means negligible issues at a time when global warming is an ominous threat to our very future,[8] and when Americans have been transferring an increasing amount of national debt onto the shoulders of

[6]James Galbraith, *The Predator State: How Conservatives Abandoned the Free Market and Why Liberals Should Too*. New York: The Free Press, 2009.

[7]Herman Daly, "Economics in a Full World," *Scientific American* 293 (2005) 3:100–107.

[8]Wikipedia contributors, "Global warming," http://en.wikipedia.org/wiki/Global_warming#cite_note-7 accessed October 9, 2014.

generations yet unborn.[9] All these issues are intimately intertwined with the economic problem of production and consumption and should not be ignored.

"Inputs and Outputs" (S&N p. 9). It is baffling that in an increasingly information-driven knowledge economy, S&N fail to even mention intangible forms of factors of production—such as knowledge. Besides the conventional factors of production there are additional important factors such as infrastructure, social capital, institutions, knowledge, human capital, culture, the legal system, and natural resources. The market could not work at all without them.

Culture is the shared belief in how the world works and members of a culture use those beliefs to make economic decisions. It has an important effect on the economy. Moreover, institutional capital constitutes the basic framework within which an economy operates and is also crucial for its functioning. The legal system provides enforcement mechanisms for laws and regulations. Institutional capital is often taken for granted by economists even though it is very cumbersome and costly to devise and take a very long time to put in place. S&N leave all this out. Yet markets do not create institutions although they interact with them and can affect them over time. This is crucial, because institutions affect economic performance crucially: they channel behavior and market processes into one of several possible paths of development. They have an impact on output and therefore on efficiency. Moreover, they can also constrain production just as the conventional factors can. Consequently, we can think of institutions as an input into the production process. Furthermore, this also means that sociopolitical processes are also important determinants of productivity. In other words, S&N's institutionless economics is misleading.

Knowledge embodied in people is called human capital. It also includes health, inasmuch as health increases productivity. The feeling of community and the network of friends and acquaintances are referred to as social capital. Social capital based on mutual sympathy, social cohesion, and shared cultural norms and values fosters trust and cooperation within the community and thereby lowers transaction and enforcement costs.

Many natural resources are essential for life (i.e., water, air, earth); they are an important input into the production process (i.e., minerals); yet many of them are nonrenewable (available in finite amounts) and many are being depleted at an accelerated rate since the Industrial Revolution. In addition, there are many ominous developments in climate change, water and air quality, biodiversity loss, and loss of ecosystems. This is a considerable problem, as the depletion of natural resources is not accounted for in the GNP accounts and global warming is a potential time bomb of mass-destruction intensity.

"Productive efficiency occurs when an economy… is on its production possibility frontier" (S&N p. 13). The PPF is not a useful concept because the modern economy suffers from endemic underemployment and the PPF is simply not within

---

[9]Laurence J. Kotlikoff. 1992. *Generational Accounting: Knowing Who Pays, and When, for What We Spend*, New York: The Free Press.

reach. The last time we had full employment was during World War II. There are other inefficiencies in the economy as well. For example, businesses find it beneficial to confuse consumers. The costs are born by the consumers. That is why the government enacted legislation in 2009 in order to reign in the power of credit card companies to charge hidden gimmicky penalties: "To amend the Truth in Lending Act to establish fair and transparent practices relating to the extension of credit under an open end consumer credit plan,…."[10] There are many hidden charges on credit card debt. Such deceptive practices ought not be considered efficient.

"Those prices for which buyers desire to buy exactly the quantity that sellers desire to sell yield an equilibrium of supply and demand" (S&N p. 27). Such an equilibrium exists only in the abstract. Sellers almost always want to sell more than buyers are willing to buy. And usually there is not a single price for even a homogeneous item. Even for such relatively simple good as milk, there are many different prices in my town. Even the same supermarket chain has different prices for milk of the same brand in stores only a few miles apart. So I am not sure what prices the authors have in mind and for which goods. Being a bit more specific would help. Price depends on two crucial variables absent from the above sentence: location and time. Even for such homogeneous items as corporate stocks and commodities the delay in reporting the latest price implies that there is no way of knowing what the current price is instantaneously. So the idea of an equilibrium price is imprecise.

"By matching sellers and buyers…, a market economy simultaneously solves the three problems of *what, how,* and *for whom*" (S&N p. 27). They do not specify how the matching is done. What is the dynamics of reaching an equilibrium? Instead, they take it for granted. The fact is that such matching is by no means trivial because producers and consumers are not in the same place at the same time and there are middle-man involved. Thus, producers have to anticipate market developments well in advance. And only on rare occasions can they do it smoothly. So there is constant volatility and turmoil which is one of the failings of the market mechanism. Hence, the basic issue is how well does the market solve these problem and what institutions can help markets come closer to efficient solutions and what safety nets are necessary when the market comes short of solving these problems?

"…in the end the major forces affecting the shape of the economy are the dual monarchs of *tastes* and *technology*" (S&N p. 28). Consumer sovereignty is an ideological concept and exists only as a myth. The reason is that S&N overlook the overwhelming question: where do tastes come from. Instead, they simply and

[10]"To amend the Truth in Lending Act to establish fair and transparent practices relating to the extension of credit under an open end consumer credit plan, …" US Congress, House, *Credit CARD Act of 2009*, HR 627, 111th Congress, 1st session, January 6, 2009. http://www.creditcards.com/credit-card-news/assets/credit-card-act.pdf accessed October 9, 2014. Wikipedia Contributors, "Credit Card Act of 2009," http://en.wikipedia.org/wiki/Credit_CARD_Act_of_2009 accessed October 9, 2014.

inappropriately assume that we enter the market as adults with tastes fully formed. This is obviously nonsense, because people are not born as adults; we enter the market as children before our tastes are formed. Instead, the development of their tastes is manipulated by Madison Avenue in the service of the business community. We refer to these as endogenous tastes. Corporations influence enormously the development of our tastes.

They succeed by repeatedly—incessantly—stressing those aspects of the culture from which they can profit. Hence, tastes are manipulated greatly by advertisement and therefore individuals are very far from being free to choose their tastes, character, and personality. We are not monarchs; we are not in charge of forming our tastes freely; we are not sovereign over their development. Instead, they are acquired from the society and the society is influenced greatly by Madison Avenue using clever psychological techniques of persuasion to manipulate our emotion in order to induce in us a desire for their products. This obvious oversight invalidates a lot of S&N's credibility.

Corporations spend a lot of money on Madison Avenue and hire many celebrities from Hollywood in order to create a bandwagon effect and convince us what to buy. So in the end there is an uncanny uniformity to our taste and consumption patterns insofar as we conform to the group ideal. We are conditioned to have similar wants. In short, individuality is anathema to the market, because firms want to mass produce products, and therefore, the advertisements are pitched in such a way as to create a mass market for goods. Thus, the market becomes a powerful homogenizing force.

In addition, the corporations develop strategies in order to incentivize consumers to spend as soon as possible, so our will power diminishes and we succumb to tyranny of instant gratification; that is how the average American became overweight and deeply in debt. Thus, we are not able to develop as autonomous human beings. The conditioning starts at a very early age. Many fast food chains give away toys for children with the meals they serve. This strategy conditions them to acquire a taste for the food of those eateries and will want to eat at those restaurants even when they no longer receive the toys.

The society also affects our tastes and behavior enormously. The Nobel Prize-winning economist Joseph Stiglitz gave a talk at the January 3, 2015, meeting of the American Economic Association the abstract of which states: "Our beliefs and even our preferences, and thus our behavior, are, in part at least, socially determined; they are affected by the beliefs, behavior, and preferences of those around us, and the position of an individual within society… There can be social contagion, where the beliefs or behavior of one group cascades throughout the economic system. This in turn can give rise to multiple equilibria: there may, for instance, be a high consumption-low leisure equilibrium, and another low consumption-high leisure equilibrium… In societies marked by high inequality, lower income individuals may attempt to emulate life-styles of the rich, leading to a high consumption society. The analysis suggests the possibility of policy interventions: by affecting the behavior of key individuals in society that are seen as role models, societal equilibria can be altered. Since individuals define themselves at least in part by their position vis a vis other individuals in society, the behavior of individuals (at the top, middle, and bottom) in societies with greater inequality may differ from those with lesser inequality—again leading to the possibility of multiple equilibria. This analysis sheds light on the marked differences in patterns of consumption and leisure that have opened up between US and Europe over the past 35 years. The analysis undermines conventional approaches not only to positive economics, but also to normative economics."[11]

S&N list a number of conditions under which markets are not efficient (S&N p. 30). However, they leave out the most important source of inefficiency in a modern economy, namely the fact that buyers and sellers frequently have different information about the transaction. This is often the case, especially if the quality of the product or service is difficult to ascertain which is almost always the case or if the product is complex such as mortgages, mortgage-backed securities, or credit cards. In fact, asymmetric information was at the root of the financial crisis of 2008 inasmuch as most of the financial products were misunderstood.

It is anachronistic for them to bring up Adam Smith's invisible hand which in the eighteenth century made bakers and butchers produce the right quantity and quality of goods, thereby increasing social welfare. However, Smith was describing an economy in which the quality of the products purchased was easy to ascertain and the transactions were repeated within the confines of a village with a sense of permanence whose inhabitants knew each other and each other's families for generations. The butcher bought bread from the baker and the baker bought meat from the butcher year in and year out. Under such circumstances, there were no incentives at all for opportunistic behavior. On the contrary, social pressure was enormous to conform to the established norms of the village. Obviously, the butcher would not have gained by selling inferior quality meat to the butcher or the baker by shortchanging the butcher. They would have been discredited if they tried to deceive, overcharge, or otherwise entrap their customers. There was no small print and the transactions were simple, repeated, and based on personal exchange. It is utter folly to compare such a market to the complex global markets of today for which none of the above conditions holds.

In short, the Smithian world of more than two centuries ago is hardly a reliable guide for today's global impersonal economy. Smith lived before the invention of the mega-corporation, before instant global communication, and before the double cheeseburger threatened our waistline and investment banks could bring down the world's financial system. The incentives are very different in a global marketplace where anonymous mega-corporations are dealing with anonymous faces in cyberspace. Clearly, people behave differently under such circumstances. In fact, there is a whole discipline, social psychology—completely disregarded by S&N, which

---

[11]Joseph Stiglitz, "Thriving Through Balance," https://www.aeaweb.org/aea/2015conference/program/preliminary.php accessed October 9, 2014.

focuses on analyzing the ways in which behavior depends on whether we act alone as an individual or act in a crowd. In the latter case, many inhibitions that are valid under normal circumstances melt away.[12]

Deceiving an unknown entity in a faraway place, one may not even have heard of is a very different psychological dilemma than dealing with counterparties in Adam Smith's village economy. When Citigroup sold some $80 million worth of mortgage-backed securities (through a local broker) to the municipality of Narvik, north of Norway's Arctic Circle, the incentives and information content of the transaction was completely different from Smith's village economy.[13] The dynamics of deception was very different in such circumstances. Citi knew much more about what they were selling than the buyers did and they took advantage of the buyer's ignorance and of course the middleman added to the confusion. In other words, bringing Smith's example of butchers and bakers in today's world is not only anachronistic but downright disingenuous.

Ignoring problem of imperfect information is like ignoring an elephant in the room. Consider, for example, the Dalkon Shield which was an ill-conceived contraceptive intrauterine device that was not properly tested before it was marketed.[14] Instead of being an effective contraceptive, the "shield" caused serious injury and 300,000 law suits were filed against the company. It is just one example where the seller's claim was not scrutinized by government prior to marketing. There are thousands more. Take *Escherichia coli.* When we buy hamburger, we do not know and do not have the capability of finding out how many bacteria are embedded in the package. So we desperately need government to inspect the meat factories because we do not want to get sick. In spite of legislation in this regard, manufacturers still try to save money and sell ground beef that is not safe to eat. Tens of thousands of people are sickened every year in the USA alone and some even die from such poisoning.[15] *Salmonella* poisoning is another example. 500 million eggs were recalled.[16]

---

[12]One person was trampled to death. YouTube, "Black Friday stampede," http://www.youtube.com/watch?v=aeSgBL7gpAk accessed October 9, 2014. YouTube, "Store Worker Trampled, Dies," http://www.youtube.com/watch?v=7aUwmsi6Wc0&NR=1&feature=fvwp accessed October 9, 2014.

[13]Mark Landler, "US Credit Crisis Adds to Gloom in Norway," *The New York Times*, December 2, 2007, http://www.nytimes.com/2007/12/02/world/europe/02norway.html accessed October 9, 2014.

[14]The US Food and Drug Administration did not begin to require testing and approval of IUDs until 1976.

[15]Diarrhea is not the only sickness. A person in 2009 had convulsions and eventually became paralyzed from consuming *E. coli*-tainted ground beef. Michael Moss, "The Burger That Shattered Her Life," *The New York Times*, October 3, 2009 http://www.nytimes.com/2009/10/04/health/04meat.html?th&emc=th accessed October 9, 2014. Gardiner Harris, "*E. coli* Kills 2 and Sickens Many; Focus Is on Beef," *The New York Times*, November 2, 2009 http://www.nytimes.com/2009/11/03/health/03beef.html accessed October 9, 2014.

[16]FDA commissioner Margaret Hamburg said that "there is no question that these farms that are involved in the recall were not operating with the standards of practice that we consider responsible," In July, the FDA started requiring large farms to improve refrigeration and do more

However, as far as S&N are concerned everyone knows everything there is to know about the economy. Modern economists refer to a situation in which one party to a transaction knows more than the other as asymmetric information. Asymmetric information is the essence of the modern economy that makes transacting in the marketplace much more precarious than was the case in Smith's time. Such markets are not efficient as a rule as was made perfectly evident during the Great Meltdown.

Another related problem also ignored by S&N is that buyer and seller may not be equally literate, smart, or intelligent. In such a case, the seller can take advantage of the inability of the buyer to understand detailed aspects of the transaction. And most of the important things we purchase in a modern economy are extremely complicated and difficult to understand and for the less sophisticated even more so. That is why the less educated often fall prey to unscrupulous businesses and are therefore at a great disadvantage in the modern marketplace.

"Governments have three main economic functions in a market economy" (S&N p. 35). No matter how much we disparage it, the government is we, or more precisely, it represents our collective will. Without it the economy could not exist. Without a legal system and effective enforcement mechanisms, markets would implode very quickly. Collectively we can do many things much better than markets. S&N forget to mention that markets are not good at protecting consumers, workers, children, the environment, the weak, the poor, protecting the rights of minorities, or the interests of future generations. Markets did not end racial discrimination; they did not enable blacks to sit where they wanted on buses, or trains, or hotels or restaurants. Have we forgotten that it was government who said that coffee must be served at lunch counter to everyone and cannot be reserved for whites? Moreover, if permitted, markets would sell cigarettes and alcohol to children. It was not until government regulation that cigarette smoking was cut in half in this country.

Free markets are also not efficient providers of health care because preventive care is a bone of contention and because individuals have biased predictions of their future health needs.[17] Moreover, there is "adverse selection"; those with the most health needs have a higher probability to insure themselves than those who think that they are healthy. As a consequence, the price of health insurance increases so that many people are unable to afford it (13 % of the population in the USA).

(Footnote 16 continued)

disease testing, steps it said would reduce *salmonella* infections by more than half. Erik Eckholm, "Egg Industry Faces New Scrutiny After Outbreak," *The New York Times,* August 23, 2010. http://www.nytimes.com/2010/08/24/us/24eggs.html accessed October 9, 2014. Britain and New Zealand, with a more effective oversight, had overall low prevalence rate for salmonella. David McSwane, "Prevention Before Recalls," *The New York Times,* August 24, 2010. http://www.nytimes.com/roomfordebate/2010/8/24/why-eggs-became-a-salmonella-hazard/prevention-before-recalls accessed October 9, 2014.

[17]Kenneth Arrow. 1963. "Uncertainty and the Welfare Economics of Medical Care." *The American Economic Review* 53, no. 5:141–149.

Besides, insurers can entrap customers with fine print that enables them to deny coverage in some cases. As a consequence, people are healthier and live longer in countries where the government plays an important role in health care (and 100 % of the population is fully ensured like in most western European countries—without deductibles).

Markets are also extremely impatient institutions and hence are not good at planning ahead. They cannot devise an energy policy that will lead to energy independence, or an education policy that will provide broad-based quality education. That is why we do not have an energy policy. Today homeless teenagers need government help just to finish high school.[18]

In addition, S&N forgot to mention that governments must establish and continuously adjust the institutions within which the economy functions. Governments define property rights and the procedures by which such rights can be exercised and enforced. Should we forget that government abolished slavery? Without government, I should think that slavery would be reinstituted.[19] Governments also need to provide safety nets; otherwise, the political structure is unstable as Maria Antoinette found out in 1789, the Romanovs in 1917, the Germans in 1932, and many other rulers who failed in that regard. Hunger is a mighty political tidal wave. Furthermore, we need government to be the lender of last resort, in order to maintain the stability of the financial system. The laws enacted by FDR served us well until they were demolished under the Reagan and Clinton administrations.

We need government to help with disaster management. Think of hurricane Katrina in 2005 which killed 1836 people and caused $90 billion in damages. The private sector was not rushing out and rescuing people. Markets are also very bad at setting and maintaining safety standards. Collective action and supervision is almost always needed because of opportunistic behavior or because of negligence. 81 people died from contaminated blood thinner imported from China.[20] Even the weight of fashion models is regulated in Milan and Madrid after Ana Reston and Luisel Ramos died in 2006 after going overboard in wanting to lose weight in order to succeed in their career.[21]

Although S&N make all sorts of assertions about "free markets" as a theoretical construct, free markets cannot exist for long in the real world. Just think of the

[18]Kevin Sieff, "The plight of the high school homeless." *The Washington Post*. December 27, 2010. http://www.washingtonpost.com/wp-dyn/content/article/2010/12/26/AR2010122602334.html?wpisrc=nl_pmheadline accessed January 13, 2012.

[19]Nicholas Kristof, "A Woman. A prostitute. A Slave.," *The New York Times*, November 27, 2010. http://www.nytimes.com/2010/11/28/opinion/28kristof.html?scp=1&sq=A%20Woman.%20A%20Prostitute.%20A%20Slave.&st=cse accessed October 9, 2014.

[20]Gardiner Harris, "US Identifies Tainted Heparin in 11 Countries," *The New York Times*, April 22, 2008, http://www.nytimes.com/2008/04/22/health/policy/22fda.html?ref=heparindrug accessed October 9, 2014.

[21]Eric Wilson, "Health Guidelines Suggested for Models," *The New York Times*, January 6, 2007 http://www.nytimes.com/2007/01/06/business/06thin.html?scp=1&sq=Health+Guidelines+Suggested+for+Models&st=nyt accessed October 9, 2014.

foreclosure irregularities that have taken place recently. Banks could not even follow legal procedures for the foreclosures. Bank of America broke into a home illegally wanting to take possession.[22] Without the right legal framework in place markets would surely go haywire. They are unstable without regulation, without a superior authority, because of asymmetric information, opportunistic behavior, and uneven distribution of power and wealth. The government has to regulate even the size of the print on ingredient labels of bakery products so that consumers are informed about what they are buying. This empirical evidence implies that it is obviously not in the interest of corporations to inform the consumer properly. How long would the securities market exist without the SEC or the banks without FDIC? It is doubtful that they would be stable for long, because fraud would destabilize the system. Fraud still persists in the current environment, but it is kept within manageable limits so that it does not threaten the system.

Governments should also be the employer of last resort. Why not bear the burden of a downturn in the economy more equitably than concentrating the burden among 5–10 % of the workforce?

The role of asymmetric information and opportunistic behavior is all around us in the economy including in such daily transactions as buy gasoline at a gas station. Note that the pump has to be controlled by a governmental agency in order to make sure that the quantity dispensed is actually the amount stated on the meter. Without establishing and enforcing such standards, the temptation for deceptive practices would be far too tempting. There are thousands of examples of the fact that markets would implode or cause irreparable damage without government interference (as the banking sector would have imploded without the Bush–Paulson–Bernanke–Obama–Geithner–Summers bailouts of 2008–09).

Competition has a positive connotation in our culture, but S&N's contention that competition is unconditionally good for society is incorrect. The reason is that there are aspects of competition that are usually intangible, hard to ascertain and is overlooked.[23] Competition can take place in multiple dimensions. It is not confined

---

[22]Andrew Martin, "In a Sign of Foreclosure Flaws, Suits Claim Break-Ins by Banks," *The New York Times*, December 21, 2010 http://www.nytimes.com/2010/12/22/business/22lockout.html?_r=1&emc=eta1 accessed October 9, 2014.

[23]Why does competition not work in eliminating such issues? The answer is simple, because of asymmetric information and opportunistic behavior. For example, suppose that some ground beef manufacturer would put a label on the ground beef stating "We guarantee that this beef has only 1 million *E. coli* bacteria per pound. We'll give you a thousand dollars if you get sick." Or "we'll pay you a million dollars if you can find more than 1 million *E. coli* bacteria in this pound of ground beef." Would people buy such ground beef? I know that I would not and I doubt that anyone else would, because many of us do not even know that *E. coli* exist in the ground beef at all, we do not know what the FDA-approved limit is, and we do not know how our acceptable level compares to that approved by the FDA. Moreover, if we want to be truthful about it, we do not want to know either and suppress it from our conscious thinking even if we have some vague notion about. All we want to know is that we will not get sick if we cook the beef properly. Basically, we do not want to consume food with any *E. coli* in it. So labeling cannot be a competitive substitute for government regulation.

to price competition alone and businesses will do their utmost to pretend to compete while introducing countervailing hidden opportunities to earn extraordinary profits along dimensions that are not easily ascertained at the time the decision is made.[24] This is the major problem with the hidden penalties of credit cards and overdraft fees.[25]

You would not know it from S&N's text but actually, information is one of the keys to understanding why competition does not lead to the kind of efficient outcomes they are so proud of. In fact, seldom have I participated in a complex transaction in which there were no hidden financial traps of some sort. The brutal truth is, to use S&N's vocabulary, that there are hardly any competitive markets left in the modern economy in the sense described by S&N in which the Smithian invisible hand results in an efficient solution that benefits both parties without government oversight. Rather, markets today are actually quasi-competitive in the sense that there is some competition along some dimensions but not along all important attributes of a transaction. In fact, businesses obviously abhor competition and this is their way to turn competition into quasi-competition to their advantage.

What is seen as governmental responsibility depends on cultural factors. The extent of the safety net provided by governments, for instance, is a cultural issue. Yet, all societies expect governments to provide some services in case of emergency such as Hurricane Katrina or the BP oil spill in the Gulf of Mexico. In some cultures, governments would also be expected to look out for future generations making sure that the society survives indefinitely. Governments are also among the most important providers of education, i.e., making sure that the next generation has sufficient human capital necessary for the complex economic system. Another role for government should be to save for a rainy day, to be able to provide for essential services from reserves in case the need arises. Admittedly, governments have not performed very well in this regard. Government reserves would be useful for Keynesian policies in case private demand falls, so that the government can stimulate the economy.

"Should someone be allowed to become a billionaire simply by inheriting 5000 square miles of rangeland or the family's holding of oil wells? That's the way the cookie crumbles under laissez-faire capitalism" (S&N p. 38). However, the cookie does not have to crumble that way at all. Inheritance taxes are under our control in a democracy. There are many varieties of capitalist economies in western and northern Europe in which laws pertaining to inheritance vary a lot. It is important to recognize that inherited wealth is a privilege similar to the inherited titles of the aristocracy which are no longer seen as legitimate. In a democracy, there is no reason why one child should have advantages unavailable to another child just

---

[24]Editorial, "The Customer Always Comes Last," *The New York Times,* August 24, 2010 http://www.nytimes.com/2010/08/25/opinion/25wed2.html?_r=1&th&emc=th accessed October 9, 2014.

[25]I was also subject to such surprises recently as I purchased something from Canada and did not know about the fact that there will be extra charges for foreign purchases on my credit card.

because the happenstance of birth. The political philosopher John Rawls argued that luck cannot be the basis of a just society. For a just society, the initial endowment of people at birth should be as close to one another as feasible.

"Conservative Backlash" (S&N p. 40). The discussion highlights well that the controversy about laissez-faire versus the welfare state boils down to one of ideology. But do note that former treasury secretary, the arch-conservative Hank Paulson was very quick to abandon his laissez-faire principles and invoke the power of the state when it came to serving his and his friends' interests by bailing out Wall Street. So capitalism remained the economic system for Main Street, while socialism was reserved for Wall Street as Joseph Stiglitz put it so succinctly.

"Markets are like the weather-sometimes stormy, sometimes calm, but always changing" (S&N p. 40). That is precisely why life is such a challenge in a free-market economy and the poorer one is the more challenging it is. The weather is not under our control but markets are, because they are man-made institutions and not natural phenomenon. If we want to improve our quality of life, we do not have to accept the roller coaster ride of the business cycle. Many other capitalist societies in western and northern Europe have enacted policies which do mitigate the negative effects of the cyclical economic downturns to a considerable degree. We do not simply have to sit idly by and accept the markets' adverse impact.

"Consumer sovereignty" operating through dollar votes determines what gets produced and where the goods go,…" (S&N p. 45). This is a common myth but one with pernicious implications, because the notion of sovereignty is nothing but a mirage. While the myth conveys the impression that the process is democratic, it is not so at all, because the dollars are not distributed equally, insofar as some people possess a lot more of the "ballots" than others. So basically the wealthy determine what is going to be produced and not the poor.

An additional problem is that because innovation favors the wealthy the new products that come on to the market creates a feeling of relative deprivation among the poor. In order to overcome this psychological dilemma, many poor- and middle-class people become indebted in order to be able to keep up with the Joneses or turn to illegal markets in order to try to keep pace. This is another reason for taking some decisions into the political realm rather than leaving it to markets, because, given the current distribution of income, markets are not democratic at all in the sense of having equal dollar votes. At least formally in the political realm, every citizen retains the right to vote although in practice a smaller share of poorer people actually does vote. Nonetheless, wealth is still much more unevenly distributed than ballot votes.

"The theory of supply and demand … shows how consumer preferences determine consumer demand…, while business costs are the foundation of the supply of commodities. The increases in the price of gasoline occurred either because the demand for gasoline had increased or because the supply of oil had decreased" (S&N p. 45). It is a pity that they provide evidence only on prices but not on quantities without which this discussion remains unconvincing. It would have been interesting to see the relationship between prices and quantities.

"The higher the price of an article, other things held constant, the fewer units consumers are willing to buy" (S&N p. 46). This is not a law like the law of gravity. Some goods are in demand precisely because their price is high. These positional goods, such as a Rolls-Royce or Louis Vuitton handbags, or diamonds define one's place in the social hierarchy. Veblen wrote about conspicuous consumption more than a century ago. Such status symbols are also called Veblen goods.

"There exists a definite relationship between the market price of a good and the quantity demanded…" (S&N p. 46). There is an approximate relationship but not a definite one. Much depends on circumstances. Suppose the price of potato chips for some reason rises above its equilibrium value. Consumers will switch eating to other products while at the same time more will be produced so there will be excess supply; As a consequence, producers will lower their price and produce less until the equilibrium value is reinstated. That is the model S&N have in mind. This is called a negative feedback loop (Fig. 1.1) because the increase in price brings about negative forces like a spring in order to bring price and quantity back to equilibrium.

However, this is not the only possible scenario. For instance, consider the increase in the price of houses that began at the turn of the twentieth century. People interpreted the price increases as an indication that prices will continue to rise and therefore bought the houses in spite of the higher price thinking that next year they would be even more expensive. In addition, they bought the houses at the higher price because they speculated that they could sell it at the higher price next year and therefore make a profit on them. Such a scenario is called a positive feedback loop in which a displacement in the price changes people's expectations and the demand curve for housing shifts to the right so that the original equilibrium is not reestablished (Fig. 1.2). On the contrary, prices drift away from the original equilibrium value. Hence, the relationship between price and quantity is hardly as "definite" as S&N suggest. It depends on the context

Again, S&N fail to provide a realistic example. Instead, they talk about a hypothetical demand schedule for cornflakes. Why talk about hypothetical demand? Why not provide an actual example? This argument seems to be similar to the method medieval philosophers used to argue their case. St. Thomas Aquinas, for example, suggested that God is perfect, infinite, and immutable.[26] In other words, if one were to imagine the nature of God in the abstract, this is the way God would be. S&N also imagine a demand curve and suggest what its nature is in their mind. As Aquinas supposes that there is a God, S&N suppose that there is a market for cornflakes without presenting any evidence. I have not seen "cornflakes" sold at the local supermarket in a long time. Instead, there is Kellogg's Corn Flakes as well as other brands. Such markets are quite different than the one described by S&N,

[26]Wikepedia Contributors, "Thomas Aquinas," http://en.wikipedia.org/wiki/Thomas_Aquinas# Epistemology accessed October 9, 2014.

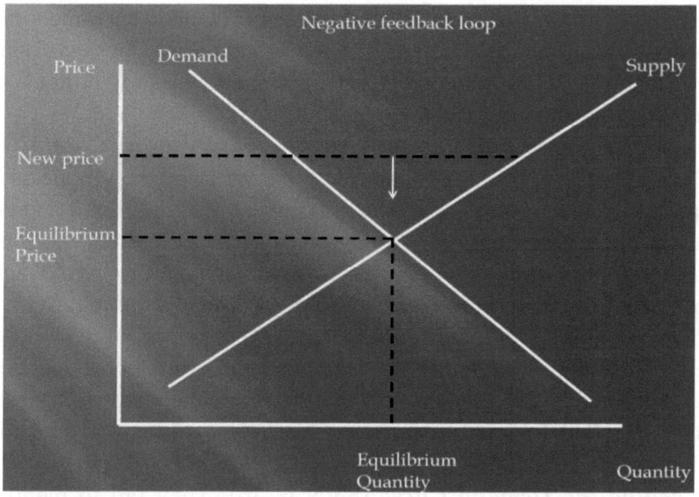

Fig. 1.1 Negative feedback loop

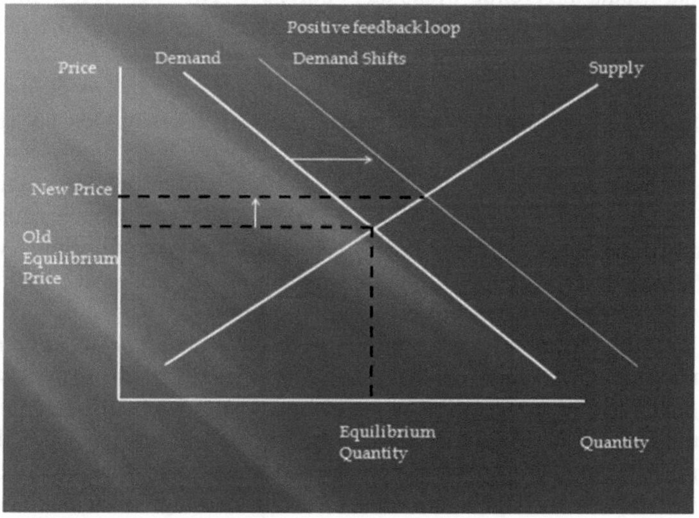

Fig. 1.2 Positive feedback loop

because Kellogg's has a monopoly on its brand of corn flakes so that market is not perfectly competitive as S&N would like us to believe. In fact, brands are the market's response to avoid perfect competition. Branded products can be advertised and the manufacturers can make various claims about their products. With generic products, firms are price takers and no firm can charge even one cent above the market price. If they were to do so they would lose all their customers. However, this is not the case with Kellogg's Corn Flakes. If they were to raise their price by one cent per cereal box, they would not lose many of their customers because of brand loyalty. Branding is one sure way of avoiding perfect competition. Businesses obviously abhor perfectly competitive markets and will do everything in their power to avoid them as much as possible.

"Both common sense and careful scientific observation; Careful economic studies…" (S&N pp. 46, 59). S&N like to use the words such as "careful" or "cool headed" (p. 78) whenever they want pretend to take the high ground and emphasize the veracity of their assertions, carefulness appears four times in the introduction and another four times up to this point. S&N obviously want to invoke authority in order to overwhelm readers into suspending their critical thinking. With so many "Nobel Prize" winners, "careful studies" (p. 33), "experts" (p. 9), "specialists" (p. 5), "eminent" and "distinguished" scholars, and even one "apostle" behind them, who is the reader to doubt the "brutal truth" of their views? Questioning is unwarranted, uncalled for, and even futile. Yet any cool-headed analysis reveals their ideological biases.

Forces behind the Demand Curve (S&N p. 46). They fail to mention advertising, the most important force behind the demand curve. It is a substantial influence on our taste, our unconscious mind, and it also conditions us to desire products that Madison Avenue wants us to purchase. They also fail to mention that what other people are buying also influences our own purchases, because of the bandwagon effect. There is a lot of copying in consumption.

"At the equilibrium price, the amount that buyers want to buy is just equal to the amount that sellers want to sell" (S&N p. 54). This may well be true on the blackboard, at an art auction, or for imaginary cereals, but I know few markets where this is the case. Supply tends to exceed demand in most cases so that stores are full of things with few buyers. No seller I know would say that she sells as much as she wants or as much as she planned to. Is the ocean in equilibrium? Well, it is not flying away, but it is constantly churning. Similarly, prices and quantities are constantly churning without ever being in equilibrium.

"Start with the initial high price of $5 per box…. At that price, suppliers want to sell more than demanders want to buy. The result is a surplus,… [and price tends to fall]" (S&N p. 55). To be sure, price would tend to fall under such circumstances, but how long does it take for it to fall is left unspecified because there is no economic theory pertaining to the adjustment time. Moreover, this hypothesis assumes that buyers and sellers are close enough to one another so that information costs of how much are being bought is available immediately to the suppliers as at an auction. However, real markets are not at all like that.

Consider that the US house prices were far above their equilibrium values for many years. After they peaked in the second quarter of 2006, they fell for years by about 30 % until 2010 and continued to linger for a year before starting the reverse the slide.[27] In other words, it took practically a decade for equilibrium prices to be

[27]St. Louis Federal Reserve, "S&P Case-Shiller US National Home Price Index," http://research.stlouisfed.org/fred2/series/USCSCOMHPISA accessed October 9, 2014.

established because people are not keen on lowering the price of their houses and taking a loss. So they rather sit on them and postpone sales until prices meet their expectations.

"Suppose that a spell of bad weather raises the price of wheat…What happens in the bread market?…a bad harvest… raises prices and…lowers quantity demanded" (S&N pp. 55–56). This is a form of callous capitalism: it overlooks the fact that lower quantity demanded implies that under some circumstances some children will go hungry and some people may even starve as often happens in underdeveloped countries when the price of food rises.

"***Equilibrium means that the different forces operating on a market are in balance***" (S&N p. 57). This analogy misses the point that prices are incessantly in a state of flux so that the concept of equilibrium gives the false impression of stability. Perhaps they are moving toward a hypothetical equilibrium but never actually arrive there. Besides, the concept overlooks the possibility that equilibrium may be deceiving insofar as forces might be accumulating within the market the same way as stresses accumulate along a fault zone in geology until the resistance breaks discontinuously and an earthquake happens. The collapse of markets is easier to comprehend with such an analogy. Catastrophe theory was developed in mathematics to analyze dynamic systems since the 1960s, but has not found its way into mainstream economics. In such a system equilibrium is a much more elusive concept than is depicted by S&N. Such a system might well appear in equilibrium for an extended period of time when suddenly, for no apparent reason, could have an earthquake-like explosion; the appearance of equilibrium was deceiving, temporary, and portended a transition to chaotic behavior.

"By determining the equilibrium prices and quantities, the market allocates or rations out the scarce goods of the society among the possible uses" (S&N p. 58). Without precise explanation on how the market accomplishes this, the claim makes it appear as though the markets have mysterious—even magical—powers to achieve these tasks. How do they do that? Abracadabra and the markets do their magic allocation. It is not at all obvious how the markets are supposed to do this seamlessly. Is there some searching involved, or is information on what is needed and where it is available free to the participants? They make it appear as though it just happens spontaneously, instantaneously, effortlessly, as the will of God. However, that is not at all the case in real markets. There are lots of problems with the way markets allocate.

Their assertion also overlooks the crucial point that the rationing with unequal income distribution leaves some people in a lurch. That may be fine as far as iPods are concerned, but not so fine as far as the necessities of life are concerned: food, health care, and housing. By excluding ethical considerations, market economics becomes unacceptable from a humanistic perspective, as it has a callous attitude toward the poor, homeless, desperate, or otherwise disadvantaged.[28] Market allocation can be cruel when you do not have sufficient funds to pay market prices for products.

[28]Being unable to take care of her two children a financially desperate unemployed women killed them. Robbie Brown, "Mother in South Carolina Killed 3 Children, Police Say," *The New York Times*, August 11, 2010 http://www.nytimes.com/2010/08/18/us/18drown.html?_r=1&hp accessed October 9, 2014.

Chapter 2
Micro: Supply and Demand in the Product Markets

"A cool-headed analysis indicates that the minimum-wage debate centers primarily on issues of interpretation rather than fundamental disagreements on empirical findings" (S&N p. 78). The actual cool-headed analysis indicates that this is a sensitive issue that turns on ideology and on which model one applies to the problem. In their analysis, S&N use a perfectly competitive model without any imperfections (in their Fig. 4.12, p. 79). Of course, that model is completely irrelevant to the current economy insofar as there are hardly any perfectly competitive markets left. Thus, an oligopolistic model would have been the correct model to use in their analysis.

Today, the low-wage employers are almost all oligopolies such as in the fast-food industry or the "big box" stores such as Walmart, Target, or Lowe's which earn a lot of profits. In such an oligopolistic market, an increase in the minimum wage comes out of profits and does not lead to unemployment.[1] Hence, an oligopolistic model would have been called for. It is as simple as that.

Besides, their own evidence indicates that the minimum wage has had no discernable effect on even the unemployment of teenagers, who are the least skilled and the most likely to be affected by the minimum wage laws. According to S&N's own evidence, the minimum wage relative to manufacturing wage was halved between 1947 and 2009 (p. 78). Put another way, manufacturing wage increased twice as fast as the federal minimum wage and instead of lowering the unemployment of teenagers as one would infer from S&N's theory (Fig. 4.12), teenage unemployment increased substantially relative to the overall unemployment rate: by about 25 %. Thus, a halving of the effective minimum wage was accompanied by a 25 % increase in teenage unemployment contradicting the deleterious theoretical effect of a minimum wage S&N described in Fig. 4.12. However, instead of pointing this out they obfuscate the issue: "There was a slight upward trend in the

[1]John Schmitt, "Why Does the Minimum Wage Have No Discernible Effect on Employment?," Center for Economic and Policy Research, February 2013. http://www.cepr.net/documents/publications/min-wage-2013-02.pdf, accessed February 23, 2013.

© The Author(s) 2016

J. Komlos, *Principles of Economics for a Post-Meltdown World*,
SpringerBriefs in Economics, DOI 10.1007/978-3-319-27828-5_2

relative unemployment rate of teenagers over this period. It is worth examining the pattern of changes to see whether you can detect an impact of the minimum wage on teenage unemployment." (p. 79) In other words, they skirt the issue and leave it up to the students to interpret the graph rather than being forthright. And a 25 % increase should not be described as "slight."

"Inefficiencies associated with the minimum wage" (S&N p. 79). S&N claim to be scientific and promised to tell the students the truth but instead they mislead and obfuscate at every turn to suit their ideology. This is an excellent example. The matter of fact is that: There does not have to be any inefficiency associated with the minimum wage at all. That is a myth. There may be, but it does not *have* to be. That makes a world of a difference. Their analysis of the minimum wage would be applicable to a perfectly competitive labor market and with full employment. Of course, if that were the case and the wage were increased, the demand for labor would decline creating unemployment. But the last time we had full employment was in 1944! That was a long time ago. In other words, the model they apply is irrelevant to today's economy.

Besides, the inflation-adjusted federal minimum wage has been decreasing and there is no evidence at all that employment has increased as a consequence. The federal minimum wage peaked at about $10 in the late 1960s (in 2009 dollars) but is now merely $7.25, a decline of some 27 %. This is so low that it is not even binding inasmuch as many states and municipalities set the minimum wage above the federal level.[2] Seattle just passed a minimum wage of $15 in the city.

Minimum wage laws basically redress to a tiny extent the power imbalance that exists in the labor market with endemic underemployment. The surplus labor implies that there is a perfectly elastic supply of workers and oligopolies can take advantage of that situation and squeeze the wage to subsistence level. Thus, raising the minimum wage merely redistributes income from the shareholders of the corporations to low-skilled workers. In today's economy in which inequality is rampant, such a policy is most certainly justified.

Discussing price controls at a time of gasoline shortage S&N suggest that: "If the free market were allowed to operate, the market would clear with a price of perhaps $3.50. Consumers would complain but would willingly pay the higher price rather than go without fuel" (S&N p. 80). It is absurd to jump to the conclusion that consumers would be willing to pay the higher price without providing any evidence whatsoever to support that assertion. To be sure, some would be able to afford the higher price but others would not have the money to do so. Admittedly, the market might work better if incomes were equally distributed but that is far from being the case and as a consequence, the increase in the price of fuel would hurt the poor much more than it would the wealthy. Again, S&N show no sympathy whatsoever to the plight of the poor. As a matter of fact, there are no poor people at all in their models although there are no less than 45 million poor in this country, hardly a slight oversight.

---

[2]The minimum wage in San Francisco is $10.55 and in Seattle it is $15.00.

S&N continue by suggesting smugly that politicians would "fret" about the high prices of gasoline. Yet, these are legitimate concerns, because at a time of national calamity it is not fair to have the rich more advantaged at obtaining gasoline than the poor for whom a rise in gasoline prices can be a painful development. Hence, the concerns of the politicians are legitimate. Letting queuing up for gasoline do the rationing is much more democratic in such an emergency, because time is the only resource that is distributed equally. In contrast, money is extremely unevenly distributed.

Obviously, letting market processes do the distribution in such an emergency favors the wealthy unduly unveiling the imbedded hidden biases of mainstream thinking. Hence, depicting government's helping the poor as "interference" (p. 79) in the free market is a distorted interpretation of the problem. Price controls on necessities such as gasoline are legitimate in a market in which there is a skewed distribution of income, particularly if other policies to redress the inequalities are not open to the policy makers.

In other words, even if S&N deny it, market processes are by no means above ethical consideration. Besides, the repeated use of the pejorative term "interference" is demeaning to what governments legitimately do to redress imbalances created by markets and to modify the unacceptable outcomes. The government is not some booby man. Actually, we are the government. It is an institution that represents our common interests. These include protecting us from those market forces that are morally unacceptable. In this instance, the government instituted price controls in order to protect the poor.

In stark contrast, S&N suggest that "Waste, inefficiency, and aggravation are likely companions of such interferences." This is disingenuous as they disregard the frustration and aggravation of the working poor if they were unable to get to work, because they could not afford to buy gasoline. Waste and inefficiency would arise with the free market solution as well. So aggravation is unavoidable. The question is how the aggravation is going to be distributed in the society and it is clear that with a price ceiling the aggravation would be more evenly distributed among the social classes. But as mentioned above there are no poor people in S&N's analysis. How can they overlook 45 million people?

"We also will learn how to measure the benefits that each of us receives from participating in a market economy" (S&N p. 84). Misleading again, because everyone does not receive benefits from the market economy. Instead, for a substantial share of the population it erects many impediments and affords only disadvantages especially for those who are born on the wrong side of the tracks, or the wrong skin color, or without an inheritance and are subsequently disadvantaged or even excluded from the labor market for lack of adequate education and because they have little to nothing to offer the markets. In other words, the market confers benefits to those who have something to offer to the markets: education, good looks, skills, talent, or money. The disadvantaged do not have any of these attributes and are therefore treated by the market as outcasts.

In addition, there are many uncertainties associated with the free market economy that create anxiety in its participants. For instance, the threat of volatility of recessions and unemployment is a major source of psychological instability. Furthermore, participants in the free market have to bear many risks as far as their education, employment, health, and retirement are concerned and this induces a feeling of insecurity that often borders on hopelessness and is responsible for many of the stresses that impinge on our life satisfaction. College students have a great deal of anxiety because they typically graduate with a debt of $25,000 and are insecure about their job prospects and about their future. So the free market economy induces many anxieties that are completely overlooked in standard treatments of the discipline such as that of S&N's.

"...utility is a scientific construct that economists use to understand how rational consumers make decision" (S&N p. 84). There goes the "scientific" hype again. However, the statement has nothing to do with being scientific; it is merely a disingenuous way to disguise an assumption. In addition, it is biased, because it overlooks the inconvenient *truth* that psychologists have proved with innumerable experiments that we humans are not rational at all. Conceited perhaps, but not rational. No less than two Nobel Prizes in economists were awarded in economics to scholars for showing definitively that consumers were incapable of being rational—not even close: Herbert Simon and Daniel Kahneman. By ignoring Simon completely and mentioning Kahneman only in passing, S&N reveal their biases clearly.

Decades ago Daniel Kahneman and Amos Tversky proved that human beings are incapable of being rational for a number of reasons including the role intuition plays in decision making. In addition, Pavlovian conditioning, cognitive limitations (IQ), and numerous biases obstruct our thinking. Our unconscious mind, discovered by Sigmund Freud, also has an important impact on our actions; yet we do not have access to the content of our unconscious mind. That means that our prefrontal cortex controls only lightly the commands that our unconscious mind imposes upon us. Furthermore, many of our choices are merely a conditioned response to a stimulus the origin of which is unknown to us. We may not know that we like McDonald's hamburgers on account of the fact that we associate them with the toys we received there when we were toddlers. Our current choice is a conditioned response to the stimulus of years ago.

Furthermore, most of us are incapable of analyzing complex problems particularly when uncertainty is involved and when time constraint is pressing. And almost all economic decisions involve some degree of complexity and uncertainty which are completely left out of consideration in S&N's trivial examples. Hence, when people were speculating that the interest rate on their mortgages would not increase, they were not even close to being capable of estimating the probabilities necessary to make such a decision on a rational basis. Instead, they followed rumors, hunches, rules of thumb, or the advice of a banker or a real estate agent who appeared reliable; some acted impulsively, intuitively, or merely copied what their neighbors were doing with dire consequences.

Kahneman has shown convincingly that in complex situations we rely on heuristics such as rules of thumb or use intuition to make decisions. In other words, our prefrontal cortex is not always in command of our decisions. Moreover, we tend to make biased assessments of uncertainty; we become confused when stressed for time, have limited self-control, and are biased toward the present. Which 20-year-old thinks that she will need a retirement income someday? In other words, rationality was not the outcome of our evolution. Our brain just needed to be good enough to ensure our survival and reproduction but we did not need to be rational for that.[3]

Human thinking is biased in numerous ways. We do not always react to the same facts the same way. Our choices depend on how the facts are presented. Such "framing" effects are important. Context matters. When an attractive model is standing by a new car, it makes a difference in our desire for the car because of the unconscious association with reproduction and we are generally not even aware of the association. There is no logical reason to associate a new car with attractive women but marketers know of the advantages of doing so. In short, context can provide stimulus to affect our mood and turn the decision from a rational to an emotional one. The inescapable implication is that preferences and our decisions are affected by irrelevant features of the product such as who is advertising it which is not rational at all.

Notice, however, that S&N's convoluted formulation does not really say that people are rational even if that is how most students would read the sentence. Instead, they state merely that that is the way economists "use" the construct; hence, their endorsement of rationality is not direct but implied. This is their way of skirting the issue of rationality but would mislead all but the most astute students and is therefore deceiving their readers. They can always claim that they are only reporting what economists think about this issue and they can report that without actually endorsing the strategy. Furthermore, they state that that economists use the concept of utility in order to "understand how rational consumers make decisions." Reading literally the statement makes one wonder what concepts do economists use in order to understand the decisions of those consumers who are not rational.

"…we assume that people maximize their utility, which means that they choose the bundle of consumption goods that they most prefer" (S&N p. 84). More than a half a century ago, Herbert Simon showed convincingly that people do not maximize a phantom utility function and received a Nobel Prize for it. Rather, he demonstrated that people seek to find a satisfactory solution to whatever problem they need to solve. In other words, we do not seek the best possible outcome—because that is too difficult and therefore unattainable for mortal souls. Rather, we seek an acceptable outcome. The two methods are very different. The best is satisfactory but that which is satisfactory may not be the best and usually is not and may be even far away from being the best. Given the limitations of our brain to process information, the limits of time available to us, extensive search costs and other transaction costs, and the myriad other impediments to acquiring information, we are content when we attain a solution that is at least acceptable to us. Trying to

---

[3]See his Nobel Prize Lecture, December 8, 2002. Daniel Kahneman, Maps of Bounded Rationality: A Perspective on intuitive Judgment and choice. http://nobelprize.org/mediaplayer/index.php?id=531 accessed October 8, 2914.

maximize would get us bogged down in everyday life, would be frustrating, and ultimately would lead to paralysis because we would become catatonic. Survival in evolutionary time required that we can make decisions quickly with little information and lot of uncertainty. There was no time to contemplate for long whether the approaching band was friend or foe; one had to make a quick judgment and act quickly. Rationality would not have helped much in such situations.

Simon called this method "satisficing" or seeking a satisfactory solution. His model is much more realistic than the maximization approach S&N assume. It is a pity that his ideas are not even mentioned even though a survey article suggests that "Psychology and economics provide wide-ranging *evidence* that bounded rationality is important."[4] It is not scientific to perpetuate ideas that have been disproven.

There is yet another serious problem: We need to distinguish between expected and realized utility. Conventional theory assumes that when consumers purchase a product, say, a hamburger for $4.30, they receive at least $4.30 worth of utility from them. This is not the "utter truth," because the item was paid for before it was consumed. In other words, at the time of the transaction the consumers do not yet know the utility they will receive from them. That utility has to be forecast. To be sure, they expect to receive at least $4.30 worth of satisfaction from them, but it may not be realized. Upon consumption, the satisfaction can turn out to be different from that which was anticipated. Hence, the amount one spends need not be equal to the amount of utility received from an item and this is another reason why income ought not to be equated with welfare. The gap between expected and realized utility may have increased over time and this may well be one of the reasons why happiness has not increased in unison with the increase in income.

One of Kahneman and Tversky's main discoveries is that absolute levels of utility are much more difficult for individuals to ascertain than changes in utility. Conventional theory claims that a smart phone will yield one a given amount of utility, i.e., that there is a one-to-one relationship between the level of consumption and the level of utility. Kahneman and Tversky have refuted this, however. Our judgment on how we value an iphone depends crucially on a reference value such as whether our peers possess one and whether we had become adapted to the use of a smart phone. In other words, the utility obtained from an iphone is not immutable. Rather, the utility derived from it is relative to a reference value or a social norm. In a sense, Kahneman and Tversky did for economics what Einstein's theory of relativity did for physics. Before Einstein people thought that time was absolute but Einstein proved that it was relative. Similarly, Kahneman and Tversky demonstrated that utility is not a constant and levels of consumption are not the conveyors of utility; the conveyors of utility are the changes in those levels.[5] So if consumers have adapted to having a smart phone the possession of an iphone would not yield

[4]John Conlisk, 1996. "Why Bounded Rationality?" *Journal of Economic Literature*, 34, 2:669–700.

[5]YouTube video, "NBR Interview with Daniel Kahneman: Your Mind and Your Money," from an interview televised by PBS on October 19, 2009, posted by "PBS," November 6, 2009. http://www.youtube.com/watch?v=rZUylXXJbhE accessed October 8, 2914.

as much utility as if they were not accustomed to having one and no one else in the society had one. In sum, the level of consumption people are adapted to plays a major role in determining the amount of satisfaction obtained from a product. This does not refer to goods that satisfy a basic need, which are essentially different. The utility derived from their consumption is absolute inasmuch as hunger and thirst has its own gauge and does not depend on external social or cultural factors. My hunger is not mitigated by the hunger of others the same way as the utility derived from the possession of iphones is.

"We know that people make mistakes. People sometimes buy useless gadgets or are bilked by unscrupulous sales pitches" (S&N p. 88). In that case, why assume that people are able to maximize utility? S&N allude to Kahneman's and Ackerlof's work in this short aside, but do not weave their findings into the rest of the text: Asymmetric information and bounded rationality are disregarded. But those are extremely important factors in the real existing economy. In the presence of imperfect information—which is to say practically always—markets are not generally efficient. And if people are hurt by predatory business practices, then it behooves us to try our best to mitigate them through consumer protection.

"a consumer will achieve maximum satisfaction or utility when the marginal utility of the last dollar spent on a good is exactly the same as the marginal utility of the last dollar spent on any other good" (S&N p. 87). Again they obfuscate the distinction between expected and realized utility. At the time people buy something they expect a certain amount of utility from that product. But forecasted and realized utility are often not the same, as the purchasers of the toxic mortgage backed securities found out. Moreover, their formulation is ambiguous. The consumer would reach maximum satisfaction at the point as described but they leave open the question whether they are capable of finding such a point.

Even more importantly, however, S&N completely overlook the fact that Kahneman and Tversky have shown that this principle is false for several reasons. Marginal utility is too difficult to ascertain, and as a consequence, people compromise and substitute a heuristic, or a rule of thumb, for this rule, because otherwise they would become catatonic. Thus, making consumption decisions in the real world is much more complicated than they want to make us believe. This holds for other marginal concepts in the remaining text. Marginal product and marginal cost are also too difficult to calculate in the real world given the limitations of our brain and data available to us. In order not to become catatonic we satisfice and aim for a satisfactory solution as Simon argued a couple of generations ago.

Indifference curves (S&N p. 101). Their description of the indifference curve is incorrect, because they assume that when deciding between two goods, say, food and clothing, it is as though we have never consumed them before. Thus, we are assumed to come to the problem of choosing in a pristine state, without indicating the amount of the goods in question we consumed in the prior period or are adapted to. However, this is inconsistent, because if we have not consumed these items before how are we supposed to know how much utility we should expect from them.

Their analysis overlooks the empirical evidence that current consumption (or current endowment) matters to subsequent consumption decisions as it becomes a

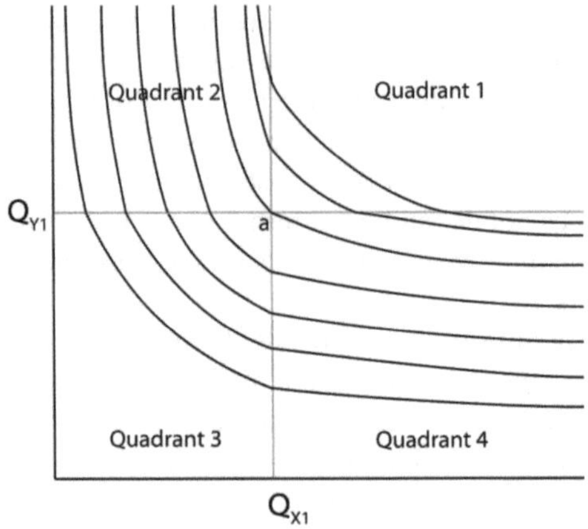

Fig. 2.1 Behavioral indifference curves showing initial endowment

reference point to which other states of the world are compared.[6] The endowment effect implies that there is an excess discomfort associated with giving something up, i.e., in excess of the pleasure associated with acquiring it. Let us suppose that the current level of consumption is (Q_{x1}, Q_{y1}) (Fig. 2.1). Then point "*a*" becomes the origin of the coordinate system and the relevant reference point for the current period.

We divide the plane into four quadrants (numbered counter clockwise) with the axis going through the origin at point *a*. In quadrant 1, the endowment effect is irrelevant as both x and y are increasing. In this quadrant, the standard convex-to-the-origin indifference curve is unchanged. However, *x* decreases in quadrant 2 while *y* increases; in quadrant 3, both x and y decrease, and in quadrant 4, x increases while y decreases. (All changes are relative to the axis that goes through the initial reference point *a*) (Fig. 2.1).

Thus, lowering consumption of (*x*) below the initial level, Q_{x1}, requires a larger amount of a compensating good (*y*) in order to maintain the same level of utility than the amount of *y* required to be given up if there were an identical increase in x beyond Q_{x1}. In other words, at point *a,* the loss in marginal utility of giving up a unit of x is larger (in absolute value) than the marginal utility of obtaining a unit of x; i.e., decreasing one's consumption from the current level is more painful than increasing consumption from the current level is beneficial. This is critical, because it implies that the indifference curves are kinked at the axis which go through point *a*, with slopes steeper in quadrant 2 than in quadrant 4, a factor overlooked in conventional treatments of indifference curves.

---

[6]Kahneman, D., Knetsch, J.L., and Thaler, R.H., 1991. Anomalies: The Endowment Effect, Loss Aversion, and Status Quo Bias. *Journal of Economic Perspectives*, 5(1):193–206; Knetsch, J.L., 1989. The Endowment Effect and Evidence of Nonreversible Indifference Curves. *American Economic Review* 79, 1277–84; Knetsch, J.L., Sinden, J.A., 1984. Willingness to pay and compensation demanded: Experimental evidence of an unexpected disparity in measures of value, *Quarterly Journal of Economics* 99, 507–521.

The budget line (S&N p. 103). The budget line is not constrained as firmly as S&N suggest, given the availability of credit cards. Most of us face a fuzzy budget constraint and that makes budgeting so difficult. That is why the USA has become an indebted nation with a median credit card debt per household of $7000 totaling about $1 trillion in total.[7] The burden of servicing such debt with an interest rate of about 15 % is obviously substantial.

"New and improved products" (S&N p. 103). They fail to note that not all new products are improvements. For instance, in the financial sector, the innovations that were hailed as making the economy more efficient ended up costing the taxpayers trillions of dollars. So they were not improvements at all. S&N discussed Pareto improvements earlier, but one important aspect of technological change that they fail to mention is that technological change is never a Pareto improvement as it always hurts some people.[8] One of the more blatant inconsistencies of economic theory is that we celebrate such a process of technological change even though it is not Pareto efficient while at the same time economists generally argue against the government redistributing income for exactly the same reason, i.e., that the redistribution is not Pareto efficient. From what derives these privileges of the entrepreneur that do not accrue to the state? In other words, according to S&N redistribution is bad because it is not Pareto optimal but innovation is good even though it is not Pareto optimal.

A major problem with our economic system is that the people who are hurt are not compensated for the losses they suffer in the wake of technological change, whereas it is not fair to have people benefit at the expense of others. Until we can create institutions which compensate the losers adequately, the economic system will not create well-being for the whole population.

"Such complex production processes can be found in every sector, from pharmaceuticals that change our mood or help our blood flow more smoothly to financial instruments that take apart, repackage, and sell the streams of mortgage payments. And most of the time, we don't even know what exotic substances lie inside the simple (recycled) paper that wraps our $2 hamburger" (S&N p. 113). The "brutal truth" is that exotic products can turn out to be toxic ones. Because of asymmetric information, i.e., the person who packages the exotic securities knows more about the product than the person who buys it. As a consequence, there is a terrific temptation that can push the person toward opportunism and ultimately deception can play a substantial role in the transaction. For instance, Goldman Sachs had to pay $650 million fine for just one such deceitful transaction. S&N fail utterly to consider this important element in exchange.

[7]Tim Chen, "American Household Credit Card Debt Statistics: 2014," http://www.nerdwallet.com/blog/credit-card-data/average-credit-card-debt-household/ accessed April 15, 2015.

[8]John Komlos, "Has Creative Destruction Become More Destructive? NBER Working Paper No. 20379, August 2014.

"Inferior technologies are unprofitable and tend to be discarded in a market economy…" (S&N p. 114). The quality of a product is not easily discernable. There are hidden qualities which do not become apparent until one has some experience with the product. For instance, the new financial instruments, i.e., mortgaged backed securities and credit default swaps, appeared to be innovations that diversified risk and Alan Greenspan and Ben Bernanke gave numerous speeches saying that they made the financial sector safer. Yet they misunderstood the risks involved and the innovations morphed into toxic assets in due course. They were very profitable until their true nature came to light. Another example is the Windows operating system. It is not and was never the best. It won the competition because of chance and an early mover advantage. Network externalities imply that early adoption of a technology can favor even an inferior one.

Again they rely on the insightful and novel example of a mousetrap. Obviously, the quality of a mousetrap is easy to discern but what about a product such as a credit default swap whose attributes are much more difficult to ascertain? Ask Dick Fuld, the last CEO of Lehmann Brothers. Actually, the business model of the whole financial system was inferior—borrowing short and lending long term—yet it is repeatedly propped up by taxpayers through the government because the failed banks were deemed too big to fail.

The development of technology is not a single event. Rather, it is a series of events following one another in space and time. The problem with the conventional view of competition leading to an optimum is that consumers as well as producers do not have perfect foresight to know how technologies will develop in the future. They are basing their current choices on current knowledge and these initial choices may lock them into a developmental path such that in the future the optimal technology can no longer be reached. According to this theory of path-dependence, the initial steps confer first-mover advantages, network externalities, such that the technology that would have been optimal but was not yet known at the beginning of the process may not be attainable. This is particularly true in case of increasing returns to scale, which means that as the quantity produced increases the average cost decreases. Most modern technologies do experience decreasing costs as the scale of operation increases. This means that first mover advantage can lock-in a technology that was not as efficient as an alternative technology that started later. It can also be that a small random event such as IBM ordering an operating system from Bill Gates can provide such initial advantages that even better technologies are going to be priced out of the market.[9] Consequently, competition does by no means guarantee that the best technology will emerge the winner in the competition if consumers and producers do not have perfect foresight or if increasing returns are in effect. Hence, Pareto inferior outcomes, i.e., socially inefficient equilibriums occur

[9]W. Brian Arthur, 1994. *Increasing Returns and Path Dependence in the Economy*. Ann Arbor, University of Michigan Press.

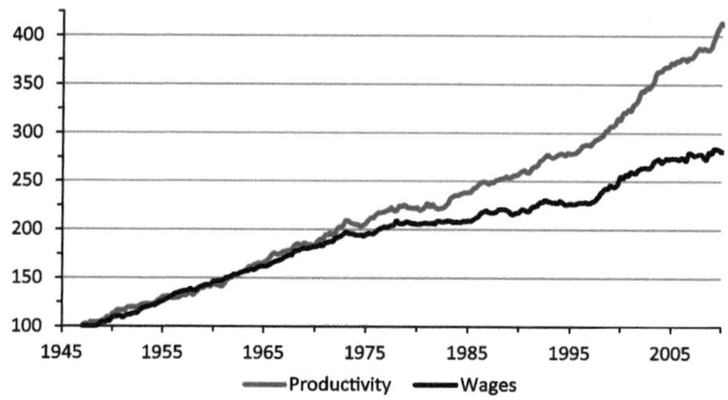

Fig. 2.2 Productivity and wages in the USA

frequently. In short, technological change is a path-dependent process that does not guarantee that the best mouse trap will be declared the winner in the end by the market.[10] S&N present a biased view that economic processes invariably and incessantly improve toward the ideal current free market economy. They fail to see the disadvantages and challenges of many developments. Otherwise, we would not have so many people in jail, so many relying on antidepressants, so many killed and wounded by gun violence, and so many struggling to make ends meet.

"…wages have tended to rise even faster than the 1.5 % percent per year attributable to total factor productivity" (S&N p. 117). This is utter nonsense. This was true in the post-World War II era while the unions were strong enough to fight for workers' wages and globalization had not yet destroyed the manufacturing sector, but has not been true since 1975 (Fig. 2.2). The fact is that real wages of men have actually stagnated since 1968 and real median household income has declined since 1999 by some $5000 (Figs. 2.3 and 2.4)![11] The only wages that have been increasing is that of women but they have still not caught up with that of men. In other words, all this praise of productivity growth fails to recognize that salaries have not kept up with productivity. That is one of the reasons why income has become so unequally distributed as profits have increased substantially (Fig. 2.5). Hence, productivity has benefited only a tiny minority people.

"The rising tide of executive compensation raises important questions about public policy…. Most economists are reluctant to have the government set any kind of pay standards" (S&N p. 122). Economists are reluctant to set pay limits

---

[10]Paul David, "Clio and the Economics of QWERTY," *American Economic Review* 75, 2 (May 1985):332–337.

[11]Wikipedia contributors, "Household Income in the United States," http://en.wikipedia.org/wiki/Household_income_in_the_United_States accessed October 8, 2914. Erik Eckholm, "Recession Raises Poverty Rate to a 15-Year High," *The New York Times,* September 16, 2010. http://www.nytimes.com/2010/09/17/us/17poverty.html?emc=eta1 accessed October 8, 2914. See also: James K. Galbraith, *Created Unequal. The crisis in American pay*. The University of Chicago Press, 2000.

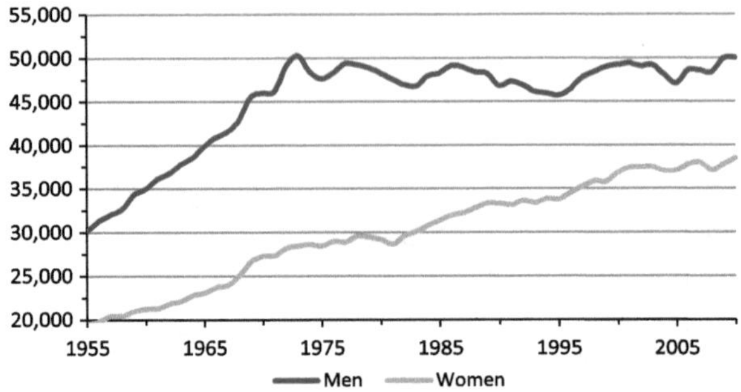

Fig. 2.3 Median income of full-time year-round workers by gender 2010 dollars

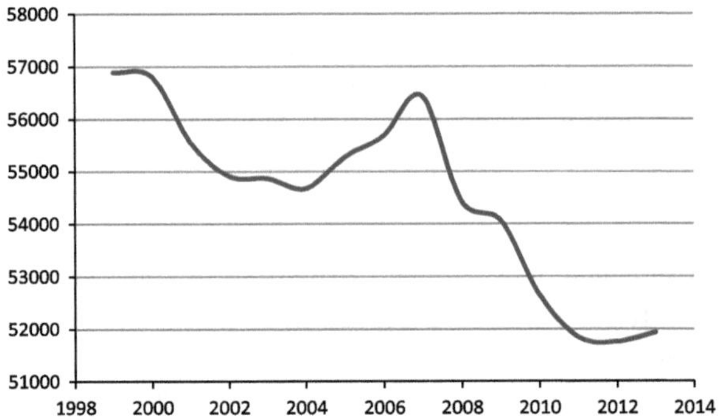

Fig. 2.4 Real Median Household income in the USA in 2013 prices

because they have a Panglossian view of the free market. They do not present an iota of empirical evidence to support the notion that capped CEO salaries would bring forth less managerial skills. Lower managerial salaries have not hurt European or Japanese firms. So capping CEO salaries at European levels would be a reasonable policy. Of course, this would not work unless it was a general policy throughout the USA. Individual firms cannot accomplish it successfully by themselves.

Those who are ambivalent about government involvement in markets might consider that the extraordinary profits and hence salaries of the Lords of Finance are possible only because they were bailed out at taxpayers' expense. The incomes earned by the likes of Lloyd Blankfein and Jamie Dimon whose annual compensation was in the $10 million range even during the bad year of in 2009 would not be as high if the market for CEOs were perfectly competitive. They are not paid their opportunity cost. After all, even those CEOs who ran their companies into the ground received astronomical figures. For instance, John Thain received $83 million before Merrill Lynch became insolvent. This evidence defies the theory that wages equal the value of marginal product.

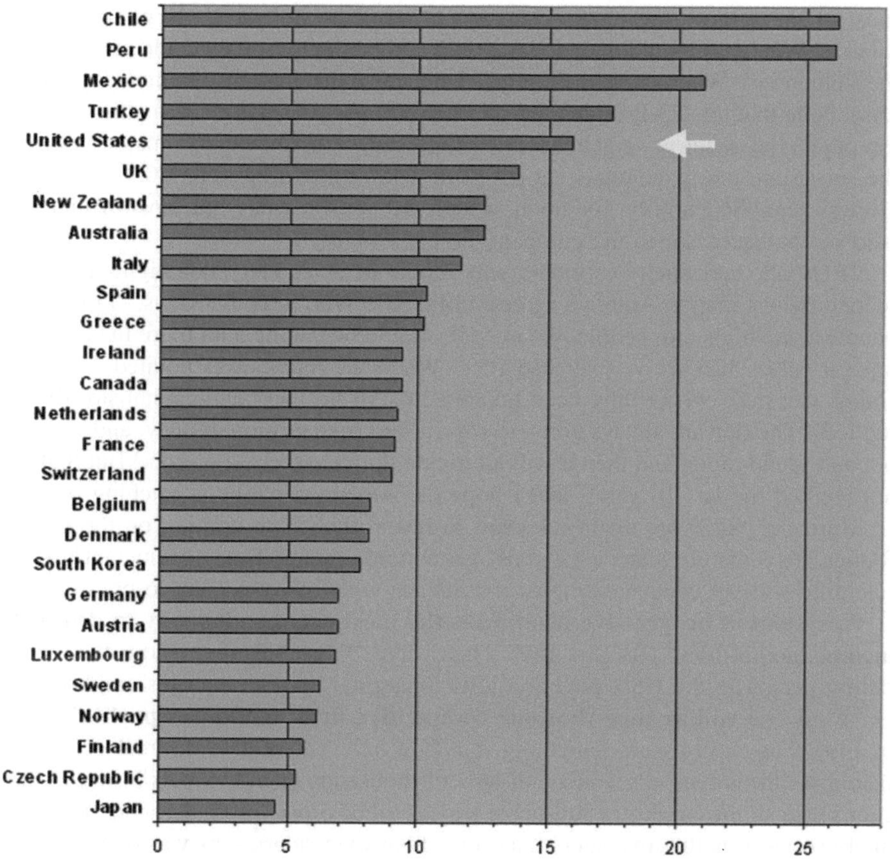

Fig. 2.5 Ratio of expenditure of top 10 % of income recepients to bottom 10 %

The reason for the high salaries is that the market for CEOs is not perfectly competitive. The positions are not advertised openly and there is no transparency on how the chief executives are chosen. Once chosen, they can essentially pack the board of directors and eventually write their own salaries. They can "hold-up" the board. If the market were competitive salaries would decline markedly, because the current salaries are way above opportunity costs. Just ask yourself if one could have found someone to run Bank of America for less than $4 million in 2009 (that is almost $2000/hour) at a time when the bank was propped up by the US treasury.[12] I bet that it could have been run as efficiently for under half a million, i.e., for one-eighth of the salary that was actually granted. The usual argument that to cap salaries would be inefficient is not supported by any evidence whatsoever, because

[12]The salaries can be found at AFL CIO, "Executive Pay Watch," http://www.aflcio.org/corporatewatch/paywatch/ceou/database.cfm accessed October 8, 2914.

most of the salaries are rents. They would work as well at 10 % of the current salaries. What else would they do? It would still be the most they could earn. Would they emigrate? Where would they go? I do not think that any inefficiency would arise. Note that the US President earns $400,000 per year. I think that should be the top pay in the country. Angelo Mozilo of Countrywide Financial, a major culprit in the sub-prime mortgage crisis earned some $450 million between 2000 and 2008. He was fined $67 million for fraud, a mere 13 % of his pay but most of that was paid by the successor to the company he bankrupted.[13]

CEOs who earn such exorbitant rents should be taxed at a much higher rate. The second richest man in America agrees: billionaire Warren Buffett says, "I think that people at the high end, people like myself, should be paying a lot more in taxes. We have it better than we've ever had it…" When the interviewer pointed to critics' claims that the very wealthy need tax cuts to spur business and capitalism, Buffett replied, "The rich are always going to say… 'Just give us more money, and we'll go out and spend more, and then it will all trickle down to the rest of you.' But that has not worked the last 10 years, and I hope the American public is catching on."[14]

Moreover, S&N are again reluctant to reveal their own opinion on the matter. Rather, they merely state what most economists prefer. Being "reluctant" is not scientific without adequate empirical evidence which they neglect to present.

"a system of progressive taxation is the most evenhanded way to deal with income inequalities" (S&N p. 149). Then why is Warren Buffet, who is the second richest person in the USA paying a lower marginal tax rate than his employees?

"First, we will assume that our competitive firm maximizes profits" (S&N p. 149). They can assume anything, but how relevant is it to the real economy? Insofar as firms typically consist of tens of thousands of individuals how can they coordinate all the employees in such a way as to maximize profits? Rather, the more likely scenario is that managers maximize their own salaries, as was demonstrated during the Great Meltdown of 2008, even if it is to the detriment of the firms. Another major problem is to align the interest of the managers and that of the

---

[13]Gretchen Morgenson, "Lending Magnate Settles Fraud Case," *The New York Times*, October 15, 2010. http://www.nytimes.com/2010/10/16/business/16countrywide.html?th&emc=th accessed October 8, 2914.

[14]"Buffett isn't the only billionaire who has argued for higher taxes. Both Microsoft co-founder Bill Gates and his father, Bill Gates, Sr., came out in support of a Washington state measure to 'create a 5 percent tax rate on annual income exceeding $200,000 for individuals and $400,000 for couples, and a 9 percent tax rate on income that tops $500,000 for individuals and $1 million for couples.'" Amanda Terkel, "Warren Buffet: I 'Should Be Paying A Lot More in Taxes," *Huffington Post*, November 21, 2010. http://www.huffingtonpost.com/2010/11/21/warren-buffett-paying-more-taxes_n_786516.html accessed October 8, 2914. "Executives Who Support Tax Increases to Fix the Deficit," *The Wall Street Journal*, October 25, 2012. Ryan Grim and Sabrina Siddiqui, "Top Two Percent to GOP: Tax Us," *Huffington Post*, December 5, 2012. Andrew Garber, "Like Father, like son: Bill Gates supports income-tax initiative 1098," *The Seattle Times*, September 21, 2010, http://seattletimes.com/html/politicsnorthwest/2012959755_microsoft_co-founder_bill_gate.html accessed October 8, 2914.

stockholders insofar as the owners of the firm are far away from the day-to-day operations of the executives and are not able to oversee it or control it. Take Dick Fuld again, for instance. He walked away from the bankrupt Lehman Brothers with some $450 million.[15] The shareowners walked away with next to nothing. Maurice Greenberg walked away from AIG with 4.5 billion in his pocket before the corporation went bankrupt.[16]

The problem is known as the principal–agent problem, a variant of "Moral hazard." People maximize their own utility to the detriment of others, when they do not bear the full consequences of their actions due to uncertainty or incomplete contracts or information asymmetries. The agent of the shareholders cannot always be held responsible for his or her actions because contracts cannot be completely specified. There are too many contingencies. In other words, there is a fundamental conflict between the manager's utility and that of the shareholders.

Adam Smith was well aware of this moral hazard: "The directors of such companies,... being the managers ... of other peoples' money than of their own, it cannot well be expected, that they should watch over it with the same anxious vigilance with which the partners in a private copartnery frequently watch over their own... Negligence and profusion, therefore, must always prevail more or less, in the management of the affairs of such a company."[17] In other words, S&N's assumption has little relevance in the real economy.

"An economy is clearly inefficient if it is inside the Production Possibility Frontier" (S&N p. 160). Economies are practically always inside their PPF, because of unemployment, underemployment, and the underutilization of capital equipment. In 2014, for instance, 12 % of the labor force was underemployed and 22 % of plant and equipment was idle. The last time the US economy was on its production possibilities frontier was in 1944 when demand for war-related production brought unemployment down to 1.2 %.

Moreover, it is well neigh impossible to structure the culture and laws in such a way as to minimize the cost of production. For instance, German pharmacies are more efficient than American ones. Why? Their task is relatively straightforward: to dispense prescription drugs. The difference is that US legal system is such that pharmacists have to register the name of the patient and have to type up a label before dispensing the drug, whereas their German counterparts are not constrained by laws to perform such tasks and therefore can provide the drugs quicker. In this case, the laws render the US system less efficient than the German one.

"One of the most important results in all economics is that the allocation of resources by perfectly competitive markets is efficient" (S&N p. 160). This is

---

[15]Wikipedia contributors, "Richard S. Fuld, Jr.," http://en.wikipedia.org/wiki/Richard_S._Fuld,_Jr accessed October 8, 2914.

[16]Mary Williams Walsh, "Insurance Giant A.I.G. Takes Ex-Chief to Court," *The New York Times*, June 14, 2009. http://www.nytimes.com/2009/06/15/business/15aig.html accessed October 8, 2914.

[17]Adam Smith, *An Inquiry into the Nature and Causes of the Wealth of Nations*, ed. Edwin Cannan (London: Methuen & Co., 1904), available online at Library of Economics and Liberty, p. 700.

also the most misleading result, because the result is almost always applied to markets that are not perfectly competitive. Moreover, perfectly competitive markets are a negligible share of the economy and consequently irrelevant for all intents and purposes. Therefore, the perfectly competitive market should not be the default model.

In the same paragraph S&N state: "we… illustrate the general principles underlying the efficiency of competitive markets." In other words, they fall into their own trap as the "perfectly" of the original statement was already dropped from the generalization and the result is applied to all competitive markets and that is how the concept seeped incorrectly into the popular mindset. Students think that competition is sufficient to establish efficiency. But that is not the case insofar as competitive markets include oligopolies and monopolies which are not efficient. Hence, they obfuscate an extremely important point in economics.

"We have seen that markets have remarkable efficiency properties" (S&N p. 164). We have seen claims to that effect but we have not seen actual evidence to support that assertion. Note that S&N now stealthily generalize the outcome of the perfectly competitive model to all markets without qualification and that is precisely one of the main reasons why such mainstream textbooks mislead millions of students. This is a pernicious oversight, because there is a world of a difference between "markets" and "perfectly competitive markets" insofar as students will be misled into thinking that all markets are efficient without exception. However, on p. 169 they themselves admit that such firms are "hard to find," and on p. 187 they do say that such firms are rare. While those qualifications do contradict the above-unqualified assertion, they do not mitigate the pernicious effect of this misleading sentence on students. Many students will retain the false impression that markets are efficient, whereas markets are rarely efficient and are more likely to be inefficient.

Furthermore, it is not only students who are misled. Such misconceptions led eventually to the deregulation of financial markets. Alan Greenspan was also misled inasmuch as he basically applied the perfectly competitive model to the financial sector that was everything but perfectly competitive. So such misleading assertions as the above are by no means benign. They have real-world consequences. Thus, the default model should be that markets are inefficient without effective government oversight and proper institutional structure, without perfect information about the product being exchanged, and if the market structure is oligopolistic or monopolistic, that is to say, practically always. In other words, efficient markets are rather the exception rather than the rule.

"People are not equally endowed with purchasing power…. So the weighing of dollar votes, which lie behind the individual demand curves, may be unfair" (S&N p. 164). Why don't we try to make it fair then? Markets are men-made institutions. Their legitimacy does not have divine origins. We can structure them so as to make them fair or at least fairer.

"Positive economics cannot say how much governments should intervene to correct the inequalities and inefficiencies of the marketplace" (S&N p. 165). If positive economics cannot say that then perhaps the theory of justice can. Or common sense, like we should all have our basic needs met before a select few indulges in conspicuous consumption. Why cannot we say, for instance, that the government, which represents our interests, should make markets more efficient? Why cannot we say that democracy trumps positive economics? That it should protect the consumer from powerful business interests as it did, for example, against the cigarette lobby so that the number of smokers has been halved? The government is not a foreign entity. It is not the enemy of the people. The government is we, and in a democratic society we, the people, have the ultimate legitimate power, and not positive economics or the marketplace.

"Sometimes it is possible for companies to create barriers to entry for potential rivals by using advertising…" (S&N p. 176). Advertising does more than create barriers to entry and not only sometimes. It always has psychological effects which create artificial demand for products we would not want otherwise. It manipulates us from the very beginning of our lives and destroys our will power. It creates a culture of instant gratification. It forms our utility function and subconscious in significant ways. Advertisements frequently use authority figures to create trust in their products. They also devalue products that you already have. For instance, by creating and promoting new fashion that has the effect of devaluing our current inventory of clothing. That means that one does not obtain as much utility from the clothing one owns as was anticipated at the time of purchase. So the new clothing destroys the value of the old.

"Branding and Differentiated Products" (S&N p. 176). Note that such brands exist only because of government intervenes in the free market and grants such monopoly powers. Without such interference enacting laws and sanctions, these brands would not exist at all and the market would be much closer to perfect competition. Perfect competition does not exist with branded products. They fail to mention that.

"Why are economists concerned about industries characterized by imperfect competition? The answer is that such industries behave in certain ways that are inimical to the public interest" (S&N p. 189). These statements contradict the assertion on p. 164 that "markets have remarkable efficiency properties." Insofar as most markets are imperfectly competitive, it is fair to say that markets are generally inefficient. Once we come to this realization then we can work on how we can improve upon them. That is the task ahead.

Consider the California electricity crisis of 2000 and 2001 in which energy wholesalers were able to "game the market" in order to create artificial electricity shortages and blackouts.[18] Enron was one of the firms which reaped huge speculative profits from manipulating the market. S&N have already forgotten what they wrote about Enron on p. 138.

"In reality many obstacles hinder effective collusion" (S&N p. 191). Moody's did not find it that difficult to collude with the investment banks to fix the ratings of

[18]Wikipedia contributors, "California Electricity Crisis," http://en.wikipedia.org/wiki/California_electricity_crisis#Involvement_of_Enron accessed October 8, 2914.

their bonds.[19] Arthur Anderson did not find it that difficult to collude with Enron to fix the books and hide liabilities. OPEC is an important cartel that colluded and dominated the oil markets for decades. But even at the local level there is a lot of tacit collusion. Consider real estate agents. There are millions of real estate agents, yet practically all of them charge a fee of exactly 6 %. One cannot find someone who would be willing to sell a house for 5.9 %. When I asked a number of realtors if they would lower their price they were all adamant about not competing with price and seemed rather insulted because such queries questioned their professionalism. In short, their collusion may not be tacit, but it is nonetheless real and is kept afloat as a social norm. It is not supposed to happen according to theory but it does. In theory, theory and reality should be the same, but in reality they are not. Economic theory does not take into consideration the sociological and psychological factors associated with competition. If they lowered their commission, realtors would be ostracized by their peers in the association of realtors and the social pressure is such that the members conform to an unwritten rule not to use price competition. It is collusion by other means. The realtors also realize that by lowering the price they would unleash a price war and others would follow suit and also lower then commission to 5.9 % and in the end they would have few advantages at a lower price.

In a market characterized by monopolistic competition firms **"will continue to enter the market until all economic profits … have been beaten down to zero"** (S&N p. 192). That outcome would be the exception rather than the rule. It would obtain only if there are no barriers to entry and only if the expected future profits are sufficiently high to warrant entry of a new firm. Those conditions do not obtain as a rule particularly because firms do their utmost to erect barriers to entry such as advertising campaigns that imply that potential competitors have to make large investments before they can become viable competitors. Hence, in reality such firms as McDonalds, Home Depot, and Walgreens all make extraordinary amount of profits which S&N neglect to mention. They also fail to mention that even if it were true that profits were zero, the market would be inefficient nonetheless, because marginal cost would still not equal price. In other words, such firms are not operating at the minimum cost possible.

"Originally… Apple… made big profits…. Today, there are dozens of firms, each with a small share of the computer market but no economic profits to show for its efforts. The monopolistic competition model provides an important insight into American capitalism: The rate of profit will in the long run be zero

---

[19]Gretchen Morgenson, "Raters Ignored Proof of Unsafe Loans, Panel Is Told," *The New York Times*, September 26, 2010. http://www.nytimes.com/2010/09/27/business/27ratings.html?emc=eta1 accessed October 8, 2914.

in this kind of imperfectly competitive industry…" (S&N p. 192). However, this prediction is ridiculous: in 2008, Apple earned $8.2 billion profits on assets of $47.5 billion, which makes its profitability 17 % and its net income has risen since then to $39 billion.[20] These profits were not competed away in spite of intense competition.

"Reducing the number of monopolistic competitors might lower consumer welfare because it would reduce the diversity of available products" (S&N p. 164). S&N concoct all sorts of rationalizations in order to sing the praises of markets. They fail to mention that reducing the number of products from which to choose might also increase welfare on account of the fact that choosing between products takes time and effort and is therefore costly. Choice is good up to a point, after which it becomes a nuisance and lowers consumer welfare especially for people who live busy lives. In other words, S&N are consistently telling half-truths. Too much of a good thing can turn into a negative, i.e., having scores of salad dressings on the shelf is excessive choice and actually detracts from our ability to make wise choices and thus decreases welfare.[21] He suggests that having "more is less," as the conventional thinking does not take into consideration the confusion created by too much choice and the time and effort needed to learn about the products offered. The market fails to provide adequate limits to facilitate our choices.

"What are the economic effects of price discrimination? Surprisingly, they often improve economic welfare" (S&N p. 193). Wow! The market can do no harm in their Panglossian view. Even price discrimination can be good…, but for whom? The owners of firms? the "brutal truth" is that most of the time it is bad for the consumers, because it takes considerable effort to elude the snares of business strategies whose managers want to charge as much as possible. Price discrimination mostly involves deception as firms take advantage of one's lack of information. They also exploit disadvantaged groups who are not in possession of a lot of information and are unable to figure out how to obtain a lower price. There is no

[20]Apple Inc.'s annual report to the Securities and Exchange Commission for the fiscal year 2014, October 27, 2014, http://investor.apple.com/secfiling.cfm?filingid=1193125-14-383437&cik=#D783162D10K_HTM_TOC783162_8 accessed April 18, 2015.

[21]"…we assume that more choice means better options and greater satisfaction. But beware of excessive choice: choice overload can make you question the decisions you make before you even make them, it can set you up for unrealistically high expectations, and it can make you blame yourself for any and all failures. In the long run, this can lead to decision-making paralysis. And in a culture that tells us that there is no excuse for falling short of perfection when your options are limitless, too much choice can lead to clinical depression." Barry Schwartz, *The Paradox of Choice: Why More is Less* (New York: Ecco Publishers, 2003). He also has a number of great lectures on video in the internet: "Barry Schwartz: The Paradox of Choice," YouTube video, 20:23, posted by "TEDtalksDirector," January 16, 2007; "The Paradox of Choice-Why More is Less," YouTube video, 1:04:08, posted by GoogleTalksArchive, April 27, 2006.

discussion about the morality of price discrimination. There is nothing, for instance, about a phone company offering one a lower price once they declined to accept their initial offer. Companies deliberately make their offers so complicated that it becomes exceedingly difficult to understand cell phone contracts or health insurance contract and compare the various plans. Companies also try to outsmart consumers by using so-called decoys which are higher priced products they are not really trying to sell. Instead, the strategy behind the higher priced decoy is to make the lower priced version seem better in comparison with it.[22] In other words, companies do not miss a psychological trick to take advantage of their ability to increase their profit at the consumers' expense.

"monopolies produce economic waste" (S&N p. 199). So do oligopolies. In fact, they should have stated that all market structures except perfectly competitive ones create inefficiencies. Hence, almost all of the economy produces waste as perfectly competitive firms are a negligible share of the economy. We could and should set ourselves the goal of squeezing these inefficiencies out of our economic life to the extent possible. All of a sudden markets do not have such great "efficiency properties."

Antitrust Law (S&N p. 203). Oligopolies should also be included in antitrust legislation in order to improve the efficiency of the economy.

"By evening out supplies and prices, speculation actually increases economic efficiency" (S&N p. 213). Nonsense! This is not the general case. S&N again present the simplest of cases in a market that is well established and people have lots of experience with it. And they fail to mention that in the case of speculation with grain when prices increase in the first period, people might well go hungry and might revolt and destroy the speculator. In other words, they have a wealthy society in mind in which the increase in price in the first period does not cause havoc. That is crucial, but they present their conclusion as though this was the case in general. However, this does not hold for markets which are much more risky, not well regulated, and investors have not had experience with them, such as with credit default swaps. Speculation in housing, in mortgage backed securities, and credit default swaps brought us the meltdown of 2008. S&N's unequivocal praise of the benefits of speculation borders on the bizarre and is distasteful in light of all the damage the financial crisis caused including a GNP which is one trillion dollars lower than what was projected if the crisis had not occurred. This GNP gap has now occurred for the seventh year in a row adding up to an inordinate sum!

---

[22] Alexis Madrigal, "Apple's Brilliant Decoy Pricing Game," *The Atlantic,* October 5, 2010. http://www.theatlantic.com/technology/archive/2010/10/apples-brilliant-decoy-pricing-game/64104/ accessed October 8, 2914.

"Reasons for providing social insurance" (S&N p. 218). There is yet another reason for providing social insurance, namely the inability of people to ascertain and believe probabilities associated with ill health and old age and therefore discount the future excessively. Young people are not generally thinking of retirement income. How many 20-year-olds are going to start saving for their retirement? Government on the other hand, through taxation, can make sure that social insurance will be provided upon retirement. Otherwise, people who lack the foresight to plan for the future can cause problems for the society once it dawns on them that their life is threatened for lack of savings. This is called time inconsistency.

"Health-care spending rose from 4 percent of national output... to 16 percent in 2008" (S&N p. 203). Lot of it is because the system is extremely inefficient. Europeans—Sweden for example—deliver better care at half the price and live two years longer!

"Infant mortality is higher than in many countries with lower incomes" (S&N p. 219). "Many countries" turns out to be about two dozen. Life expectancy in the USA is at the level of Cyprus (Fig. 2.6). Canadians and Australians can expect to live three full years longer. The health care sector provides a good example of the failure of markets to provide efficient services. There is a lot of price gauging on account of the lack of price competition among hospitals and doctors and asymmetric information between doctors and patients (Fig. 2.7). Doctors can take advantage of patients' lack of information in order to increase their own income. It is not efficient to organize the health care sector as a business enterprise.

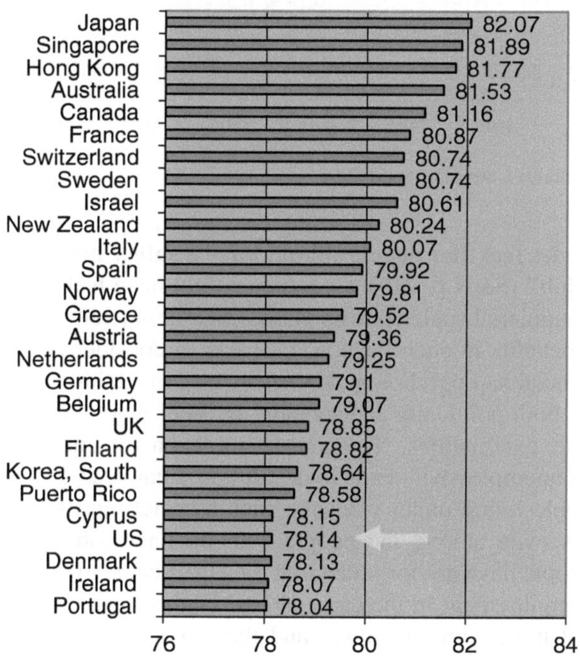

Fig. 2.6 Life Expectancy at Birth, 2008

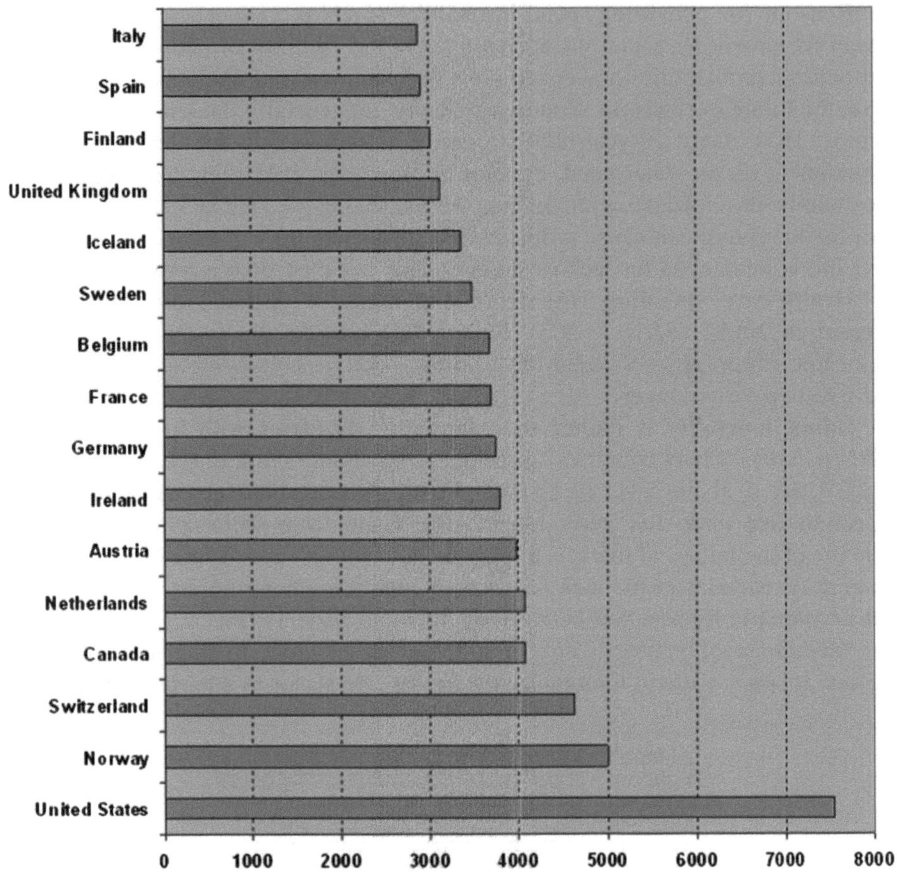

Fig. 2.7 Cost of Health Care per capita 2008

"some countries feel that people should have a safety net under them should they lose their job" (S&N p. 219). Countries do not have feelings. It is the people in all advanced industrial societies who choose in a democratic manner to structure unemployment benefits in such fashion. One has to consider also that unemployment causes financial and psychological distress and, in addition, has a destabilizing effect on society both politically and socially. In other words, the unemployed also produce negative externalities. The anti-social behavior includes break-ins, or robberies, and if unemployment ends in destitution it can lead to foreclosed houses, or homeless people living under viaducts; such a society leads to a sense of insecurity and stress even among the people who do have jobs. And of course, in Europe many people have not forgotten that the Nazis came to power because of the steep rise in unemployment in the early 1930s. Without the Great Depression, the Nazis would not have come to power and there would not have been a Second World War.

"rapid growth of expenditures on medical care" (S&N p. 203). It has also grown because the American Medical Association is a powerful cartel that limits the supply of doctors. It is rather odd that the USA can produce everything else in abundance but is unable to produce as many doctors per capita as other rich societies. The well-kept secret is that the American Medical Association (AMA) has been very successful in quietly restricting medical education in the name of fostering excellence in medical care. But that is a pretext. The real reason is to inflate doctors' salaries well above competitive levels.

Other countries have been able to cap costs because they have adopted a more efficient health care system. It is much more convenient and efficient to have a single not-for-profit entity organizing the medical system than navigating through the confusing offerings of a free market for-profit system. The former is much less expensive because the administrative costs are much lower and costs are kept down by the bargaining power of government so that medical care does not become a business and no profits are generated. S&N are great supporters of efficiency yet fail to see that the US health care system is among the most inefficient in the world.

"Health care is an economic commodity like shoes and gasoline" (S&N p. 221). This is nonsensical. Health care is a basic need that completely different from the other products. Running out of gas can well be an inconvenience but it is nonetheless on a different level of misery from seeing people suffer from an ailment, particularly if they could have been treated if they had the money for medical care. Theirs is an ideologically loaded perspective, because there are others who think that health care is a human right that does not have to be rationed in a way that shoes have to be rationed. For one thing, medical care it is not subject to fashion changes as are shoes; X-rays are not likely to become trendy. Moreover, it is not an exhaustible resource as is oil from which gasoline is derived and does not pollute as gasoline does. I have not heard of anyone wanting to get a lung X-ray when it was unnecessary. However, I have heard of doctors ordering X-rays when they were unnecessary.

In fact, 3 of the 8 Millennium Development Goals of the United Nations pertain to health: child health, maternal health, and combatting diseases. I guess S&N do not know that Article 23 of the Universal Declaration of Human Rights of the United Nations states that "Everyone,… has the right to social security" and Article 25 states that "Everyone has the right to a standard of living adequate for the health and well-being of himself and of his family, including food, clothing, housing and medical care and necessary social services, and the right to security in the event of unemployment, sickness, disability, widowhood, old age or other lack of livelihood in circumstances beyond his control." Mothers and children are singled out for being "entitled to special care and assistance." However, gasoline is not mentioned as a human right while health is one of the more important ones. Thus, attempting to conflate these three very different kinds of goods/services obfuscates their actual importance to real human beings rather than virtual people on the blackboard.

"Physicians' services, nursing care, hospitalization, and other services are limited in supply" (S&N p. 221). But the supply should and could be the amount required to keep the population healthy. S&N overlook the role of the AMA in restricting supply and competition in the name of fostering excellence in medical care (see Footnote 15). By restricting the number of students of medicine, the AMA inflates doctors' salaries well above competitive levels. Only half of those applying to medical schools are accepted. In spite of the shortage of doctors, the medical profession is opposing foreign medical schools sending their students to the USA for internships (see Footnote 16). There are only 140 accredited medical schools in the country as compared to 200 law schools. Consequently, US doctors earn five times as much as their Japanese colleagues. I doubt seriously that they are five times more productive.

It is rather odd that the USA can produce all other professions in abundance but is unable to produce as many doctors (per capita) as other advanced industrial societies (see Footnote 17). Compared to Austria's 4.6 and Norway's 4.0, the USA has only 2.6 doctors per 1000 of its population. In order to increase the number of physicians per capita to Norway's level, the number of doctors in the USA would have to be increased by some 480,000. Compared to the 750,000 physicians in the USA currently, this would be a 60 % increase.

Because of the artificial shortage created by the AMA, the income of doctors is well above the competitive level. In other words, the high earnings of US doctors are not brought about by market forces; they are not predicated only on their investment in education, but by the fact that the institutional structure protects doctors from market forces. In short, the AMA has been much more effective than other organizations in maintaining the salaries of its members well above competitive levels by restricting supply (see Footnote 18). Already decades ago Milton Freedman called the AMA the strongest trade union in the country.

Moreover, the demand for health care is not as price sensitive as S&N depict in their Fig. 11-3. In fact, the demand for most services is perfectly inelastic. Who would fill a cavity in their tooth unless there was one, or put a cast on their hand unless it was broken? Hence, all the worry about abuse of the system is unwarranted. The system should not be designed for hypochondriacs.

Chapter 3
Micro: Supply and Demand in the Factor Markets

"there are more self-made men and women today than there were a decade ago" (S&N p. 229). There are also more poor people and more people on food stamps than there were a decade ago. The recession induced "a large expansion in the share of households with zero or negative net worth from 18.6 to 24.1 %."[1] In other words, a quarter of households own nothing but debt.

The myth of the "self-made" individual is widespread in America but is exaggerated as Malcolm Gladwell cogently argues.[2] Actually, there are few self-made men or women because one's career path has a lot to do with external circumstances, luck, or innate talent which is not under the individual's control. It appears like Bill Gates were a self-made man, but the fact is that he had a privileged start in life. His parents were wealthy enough to enroll him in an exclusive high school which happened to have a mainframe computer available for its students. How many 13 year olds in 1968 had such a break in life? Gates was obviously talented and intelligent and had considerable entrepreneurial savvy, but he was born with these attributes. Certainly, to his credit, he did build on them and took advantage of the opportunities they provided, but he did not create those basic attributes without which he would not have succeeded. Thus, he was fundamentally not a "self-made man." He was the beneficiary of the lucky circumstances of his birth and made something of them. He got his break through his parents and school, and the IT revolution that was in progress. He also benefited greatly from the luck that IBM's negotiations with a potential provider of a personal computer operating system broke down so that IBM approached Gates who ultimately provided them with a program most of which he did not write himself but served more or less as a middleman. Moreover, his wealth is by no means proportional to his the effort he expanded.

[1]Edward N. Wolff, 2010. Recent Trends in Household Wealth in the United States: Rising Debt and the Middle-Class Squeeze—an Update to 2007. Levy Economics Institute of Bard College, March. Working Paper No. 589. http://www.levyinstitute.org/publications/?docid=1235 October 8, 2014.

[2]Malcolm Gladwell, *Outliers: The Story of Success*. Little, Brown, and Co. 2008.

© The Author(s) 2016

J. Komlos, *Principles of Economics for a Post-Meltdown World*,
SpringerBriefs in Economics, DOI 10.1007/978-3-319-27828-5_3

There are other reasons for doubting the "self-made" myth, because previous generations have created and endowed us with the means of pursuing our activities. And none of us in the USA, including Bill Gates, would have the opportunities we have now, if it were not for the thousands of teenage boys who sacrificed for us on Utah and Omaha Beaches or at Yorktown or the thousands who never got to see the top of Monte Cassino. These were not uncommon events. The list could be expanded by the thousands. We tend to forget the sacrifices of prior generations that enable us to benefit from the opportunity sets of today. We can never repay that. We should, however, appreciate it sufficiently so as to pass the torch to the following generations. Unfortunately, our history lessons failed to make this clear to S&N. Let us not kid ourselves that we did it or do it all by ourselves, and therefore, we deserve all the rewards we can get our hands on. It is just a lot of hubris.

Similarly, the Lords of Wall Street would not be raking in the billions if it were not for the Internet and satellites created primarily at government's initiative and expense and made available to the market free of charge. Those who rail against government interference in the marketplace should take into consideration that their privileges, and extraordinary profits are possible only because the taxpayers have created an infrastructure that is available to them free of charge.

The same argument applies to the sports millionaires. Their salaries are derived through the use of public goods such as stadiums, the Internet, and airwaves. Without their ability to tap into those public goods, their salaries would not be much above those earned by the average worker. Their salaries are not predicted by their achievements alone. Moreover, if sport is to be treated as a privileged industry and be exempt from antitrust legislation, the people who participate in sports should not reap the benefits of that legislation. Without these laws, LeBron James and Kobe Bryant would not be earning $17 and $28 million, respectively. Their salaries are not the product of free-market supply-and-demand forces but of the laws that allow the National Basketball Association to effectively be a cartel. The whole structure of mega-sports is built on a foundation of government-sanctioned privilege that protects the teams from competition and allows them to have monopoly power. Of course, they can earn extraordinary salaries from these monopoly rights. Is that privilege for sports fair? Even if this might be a reasonable way to organize sports, there is no reason why the players or the franchises should profit from the legislation. Their salaries are not the outcome of their achievements alone.

"Why is Bill Gates worth $60 billion while half of American black families have net worth less than $20 thousand?" (S&N p. 229) That is something that I would like to know myself. I find it ridiculous that they keep on posing such questions without answering them. I would love to hear their opinion. Gladwell's answer is that Gates' success was not the outcome of free-market forces but a combination of a privileged start in life coupled with talent, determination, and a good dose of luck. John Rawls, a political philosopher of justice, would certainly not consider it a just reward for Gates' de facto contributions to the economy. Besides, Gates' ancestors were not slaves who did not paid for their work and therefore could not accumulate wealth that could be passed on to subsequent generations.

S&N could have also mentioned that the top 1 % of households own about a third of the total wealth in the USA and that the bottom 20 % of households have negative net wealth, that is to say, they have more debts than assets.[3] And the second quintile has a meager $7000 net wealth and that includes TV sets, furniture, automobiles, clothing, and everything else. In other words, the first two quintiles taken together, the bottom 40 % of households—or about 120 million people—have a net wealth of $1000 which means that they own a few pieces of furniture and perhaps a TV set. Actually, the data on the black families must be outdated because in 2011, the bottom 60 % of black household's net wealth was $4500. In other words, the bottom 60 % of black households owned nothing but debt on average.[4]

"Why are some people paid $10 million a year, while others net only $1 an hour?" (S&N p. 229) It is absurd to keep on posing such questions without answering them. I have no idea who would be earning $1 per hour, because even waitresses get $2.25 plus tips. Perhaps they have a Chinese worker in mind. Turning to the other end of the income spectrum, my view of the exorbitant salaries of CEOs is that their contribution to their firms is hardly worth the millions they receive. They receive such exorbitant salaries only because they are able to capture substantial rents from the extraordinary profits of the company. They are basically writing their own checks. Warren Buffett, one of the most consistently successful of contemporary investors, describes the process by which CEOs are able to obtain astronomical salaries: "Accountability and stewardship withered in the last decade, becoming qualities deemed of little importance by those caught up in the Great Bubble. As stock prices went up, the behavioral norms of managers went down. By the late '90s, as a result, CEOs who traveled the high road did not encounter heavy traffic.... Too many of these people, however, have in recent years behaved badly at the office, fudging numbers and drawing obscene pay for mediocre business achievements. These otherwise decent people simply followed the career path of Mae West: 'I was Snow White but I drifted.' In theory, corporate boards should have prevented this deterioration of conduct... 'If able but greedy managers overreach and try to dip too deeply into the shareholders' pockets, directors must slap their hands...' over-reaching has become common but few hands have been slapped. Why have intelligent and decent directors failed so miserably? The answer lies... in what I'd call 'boardroom atmosphere.' when the compensation committee —armed, as always, with support from a high-paid consultant—reports on a megagrant of options to the CEO, it would be like belching at the dinner table for a director to suggest that the committee reconsider... My own behavior, I must ruefully add, frequently fell short as well: Too often I was silent when management made proposals that I judged to be counter to the interests of shareholders. In those cases, collegiality trumped independence... In recent years compensation

---

[3]Marina Vornovitsky, Alfred Gottschalck, and Adam Smith, "Distribution of Household Wealth in the U.S.: 2000 to 2011." U.S. Census Bureau press release, March, 2013. https://www.census.gov/people/wealth/files/Wealth%20distribution%202000%20to%202011.pdf accessed April 19, 2014.

[4]U.S. Census Bureau, Wealth and Asset Ownership, https://www.census.gov/people/wealth/data/disttables.html accessed April 19, 2015.

committees too often have been tail-wagging puppy dogs meekly following recommendations by consultants, a breed not known for allegiance to the faceless shareholders who pay their fees... This costly charade should cease."[5]

This sounds quite convincing. This is not a chalkboard economist writing. This is not an anti-globalization radical, but a billionaire who made all his money in the free market and has seen at firsthand the way typical board of directors functions. Buffett also has enough common sense to realize that the $10-million-a-year CEO basically dips into shareholders' pockets.

Contradicting S&N's insinuation of above, Buffett also said that, "My luck was accentuated by my living in a market system that sometimes produces distorted results, though overall it serves our country well... I've worked in an economy that rewards someone who saves the lives of others on a battlefield with a medal, rewards a great teacher with thank-you notes from parents, but rewards those who can detect the mispricing of securities with sums reaching into the billions. In short, fate's distribution of long straws is wildly capricious."[6] Consequently, I would have appreciated greatly S&N's explanation for why people earn $10 million while others earn only $1.

"Questions about the distribution of income are among the most controversial to economics" (S&N p. 229). No wonder the share of the top 1 % of income earners has increased between 1982 and 2006 from 13 to 21 % of total income, whereas the share of the bottom 40 % has declined from 12 to 9 % total income.[7] I would call that an obscenely unfair distribution. That can in no way reflect the social value of what these workers are producing.

"The share of national income going to labor has changed very little since 1970. This is one of the remarkable features of the income distribution in the United States" (S&N p. 231). It is more than remarkable, because it is misleading on account of the fact that the incomes of the Lords of Wall Street and other CEOs are included in the labor statistic inasmuch as they are considered employees and their income is therefore labor income! In other words, the incomes of Lloyd Blankfein, James Dimon, Walid Chammah, and John Havens whose annual salary and bonuses (in 2009) were in the $10 million range, and of John Stumpf and Thomas Montag who earned two-three times as much (all of it at taxpayer's largess by the way as a direct outcome of the bailouts), are conflated with the

---

[5]Warren Buffett, Chairman of the Board, letter "To the Shareholders of Berkshire Hathaway, Inc." February 21, 2003, http://www.berkshirehathaway.com/letters/2002pdf.pdf accessed October 8, 2014.

[6]Wikipedia, "Warren Buffett," http://en.wikipedia.org/wiki/Warren_Buffett#Expensing_of_stock_options accessed October 8, 2014.

[7]Edward N. Wolff, 2010. "Recent Trends in Household Wealth in the United States: Rising Debt and the Middle-Class Squeeze—an Update to 2007." Levy Economics Institute of Bard College March Working Paper No. 589. http://www.levyinstitute.org/publications/?docid=1235 accessed October 8, 2014.

minimum-wage earning hamburger flippers at McDonald's.[8] I do not think that CEO salaries are labor incomes in the conventional sense. Rather, they are rents which they are able to extract from the profits of the corporations, as a consequence of the weaknesses of corporate governance in the USA. Germany and Japan have pretty good CEOs yet their salaries are a fraction of that earned by their counterparts in the USA.

In addition, labor's share of national income has declined substantially in the US contrary to S&N's assertion in spite of the biases introduced by the CEO salaries. Labor's share peaked at 67.6 % in 1974 and at 66 % in the year 2000, but by 2009, the writing of their book, it was down to 62.6 %, a decline of some 5 %.[9] For each percentage decline, labor loses some $160 billion. Thus, the total decrease of labor's share was about $800 billion. These losses to labor income are substantial and again biased downward because they include the labor income of CEO's. The decline continued after 2009 and was down to 62.2 % in 2011.

In any event, by itself that statistic does not give us a good indication of the changes in the distribution of labor income. Between 1982 and 2006, the earnings of the top 1 % of the labor force increased from $800,000 to about $1.8 million, an increase of some 127 %. In the meanwhile, the earning of the bottom 40 % of the labor force increased from $19,000 to $20,000, an increase of a mere 7 %. In 1982, the former was earning 42 times that of the latter, while by 2006, the multiple rose to 88.[10] It is not likely that S&N have the tools to explain these developments as they are more likely found in the decline in the unions which tipped the balance of power in favor of big business and in government policy which basically abandoned the interests of the working class. Government deregulation and globalization tended to destroy the power of labor to extract a fair share of profits which then accrued instead to the few at the top of managerial hierarchy. This was a concerted effort to redistribute income in favor of the well to do and was not brought about by market forces alone. In fact, the managers were able to increase their salaries by protecting themselves from market forces. In addition, globalization meant that unskilled labor in the USA had to compete with low-wage workers in the developing world, especially in China.

"Going into supply and demand is just the first step on the road to understanding income distribution in a competitive market economy" (S&N p. 233). Again, the word "perfectly" is missing from this sentence also. It is true for a perfectly competitive economy, but it is not true otherwise as they themselves argue on pp. 160 and 189. Note that the market for CEOs is far from being perfectly

[8]Of Goldman Sachs, JPMorgan Chase, Morgan Stanley, Citigroup, Wells Fargo, and Bank of America, respectively. AFL-CIO, "Executive Paywatch. High-Paid CEOs and the Low-Wage Economy," http://www.aflcio.org/corporatewatch/paywatch/ accessed October 8, 2010.

[9]St. Louis Federal Reserve, "Share of Labour Compensation in GDP for the United States," http://research.stlouisfed.org/fred2/series/LABSHPUSA156NRUG# accessed October 4, 2014.

[10]Edward N. Wolff, 2010. Recent Trends in Household Wealth in the United States: Rising Debt and the Middle-Class Squeeze—an Update to 2007. Levy Economics Institute of Bard College March Working Paper No. 589. http://www.levyinstitute.org/publications/?docid=1235 accessed October 8, 2010.

competitive as they are basically able to carve out a chunk out of profits for themselves by writing their own checks. According to the most recent estimates, about a third to a half of the salaries in the financial sector are actually rents and this pertains to all employees not only to CEOs. The authors conclude that "financiers are overpaid" and that most of the super-salaries was associated with the deregulation of the financial industry.[11] The share of rent is much higher for the top management. (S&N discuss such rents on pp. 256 and 269).

Even those CEOs who ran their companies into the ground CEOs earn astronomical salaries. This is true of people like John Thain who succeeded Stanley O'Neal the year before Merryl Lynch went bankrupt and earned some $83 million, James Cayne who bankrupted Bear Stearns, Angelo Mozilo who bankrupted Countrywide Financial, and Dick Fuld, the CEO, who ran Lehmann Brothers into the ground but who nonetheless walked away with around $450 million.[12] In other words, they are all rich although none of them did a good job as CEO. O'Neal left the firm in bad shape but still received a severance package of $161 million in addition to his salary in 2006 of $91 million. And the list could be extended ad infinitum.[13] In other words, S&N insinuation that the competitive market is working in the labor market is utter nonsense.

Today, a CEO earns about 350 times the earnings of an average worker. In 1980, the comparable ratio was closer to 50.[14] Does that have anything to do with supply and demand for CEOs? Would S&N argue that the productivity of CEOs increased by a factor of 7 relative to the rest of the workforce? I find that extremely unlikely. It did not increase as much in other countries. In a perfectly competitive economy, there would not be such discrepancies in earnings.

Why are surgeon's salaries so high? **"The supply of surgeons is severely limited by the need for medical licensing and the length and cost of education and training"** (S&N p. 240). They forget to mention the crucial fact that the supply is also limited by nonmarket forces, namely by the American Medical Association (AMA) which already Milton Freedman called the strongest trade union in the country.[15] Surgeon's salaries are a bad example of how the market determines incomes in as much as the supply is constrained by the AMA and is not in perfect

---

[11]Phillippon, Thomas and Reshef, Ariell, 2009. "Wages and Human Capital in the U.S. Financial Sector: 1909–2006," NBER Working Paper no. 14644. http://www.nber.org/papers/w14644 accessed October 8, 2010.

[12]The amount is in dispute. He claimed that the figure was closer to $300 million.

[13]Consider Douglas Ivester, the CEO of Coca-Cola Co. in the late 1990s. In 1999, its shareholders lost about $22.5 billion, or about 14 % of their stake. Notwithstanding, Mr. Ivester earned some $74 million during the same year. Gian Luca Clementi and Thomas F. Cooley, 2009. "Executive Compensation: Facts." NBER Working Paper 15426, http://www.nber.org/papers/w15426 accessed October 8, 2010.

[14]Sarah Anderson, John Cavanagh, Chuck Collins, Sam Pizzigati, and Mike Lapham, Executive Excess 2008 (Washington, DC: Institute for Policy Studies and United for a Fair Economy, 2008); G. William Domhoff, Wealth, Income, and Power, at the site Who Rules America? www2.ucsc.edu/whorulesamerica/power/wealth.html accessed October 8, 2014.

[15]http://wallstreetpit.com/5769-the-medical-cartel-why-are-md-salaries-so-high.

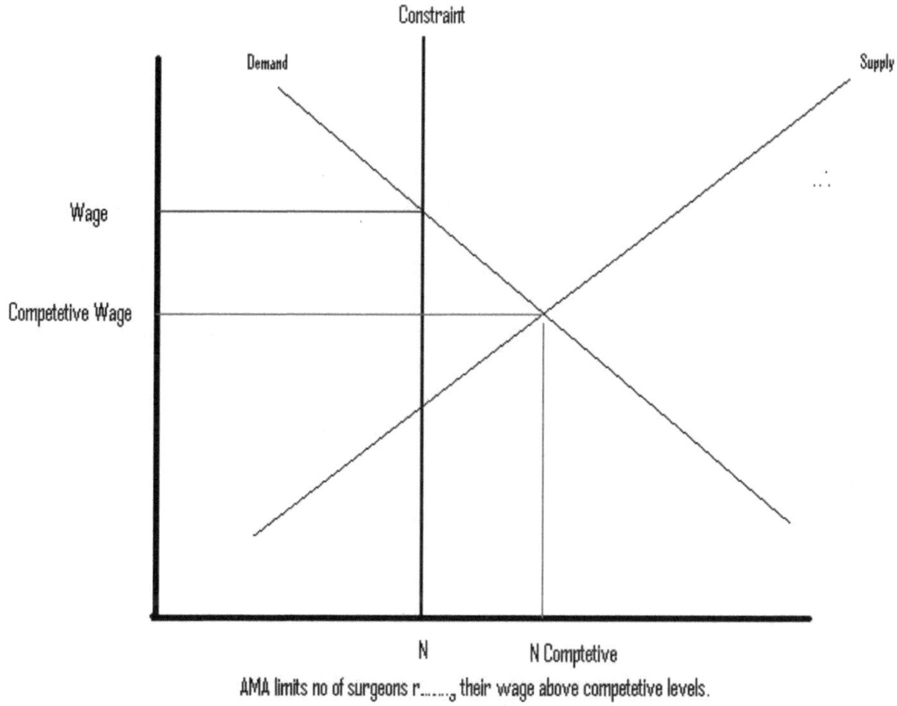

Fig. 3.1 The American Medical Association limits the number of doctors to N in order to raise doctors' salaries

competitive equilibrium determined by market forces alone. Rather, their salaries are determined by the institutional structure of the economy, i.e., the power of the AMA to limit supply. Competition is anathema to anyone wanting to make a profit, and organizations will do their best to avoid competition. With the AMA constraining the number of surgeons to N, there are fewer surgeons than there would be in competitive equilibrium and the wage is above the competitive wage (Fig. 3.1).

"Individual incomes are determined by underlying market forces" (S&N p. 241). This may be true for low-skilled workers at Wal-Mart but certainly not so at the top of the organization where salaries are determined by bargaining and not by a perfectly competitive market. There is not a functioning market for CEOs. Such positions are not advertised. Instead, such salaries are determined in boardrooms as Buffett explained above.

Furthermore, many additional salaries are determined administratively outside of the markets. All government employees are in that category, and there are nearly 20 million of them including teachers, firemen, military, and policemen. Their salaries are determined within a bureaucratic system. Their marginal product is impossible to determine.

"Suppose a smooth production function relates Q to labor and capital..." (S&N p. 243) "Supposing" does not sound too scientific. It is pretty simple blackboard economics just to assume that it is so. But suppose the production function is not smooth. Suppose there is one machine and one person running it. The addition of a machine will not contribute to output and the addition of a worker will also not increase output. So how would S&N distribute the joint product created by the teamwork of the machine and worker? The marginal principle does not help in this case. S&N also fail to provide evidence that the production function is smooth.

"In competitive markets, the demand for inputs is determined by the marginal products of factors" (S&N p. 243). Again this is a false statement, because they neglected to add that this is true only in perfectly competitive markets, but not otherwise. Moreover, for many occupations, such as teachers, policemen, and soldiers, the marginal product cannot be calculated in principle. In such cases, bureaucrats use a heuristic or rule of thumb or follow a convention in order to determine salaries. With so many people working in occupations whose marginal product's value is in principle undefined, the rest of the labor market is distorted anyhow so that even if we could measure marginal product, it would not be accurate.

In traditional theory, firms pay wages equal to the value of marginal product. Accordingly, real wages should keep pace with productivity. Yet this conjecture is easy to refute, because wages have not kept pace with productivity at all since 1970 (Fig. 3.2). Between 1947 and 1970, there was no difference between productivity growth and the growth in real wages, just as theory predicted; both almost doubled in the intervening quarter century, growing at an annual compounded rate of 2.7 %.

After 1982, however, a substantial productivity–wage gap developed: While productivity picked up to 2.2 % per annum, real wages lagged far behind, increasing at less than half that rate (1.0 %) (Table 3.1). This implied that productivity increased by 85 % during the following three decades, while wages increased by just 35 %. The divergence is an obvious contradiction of the

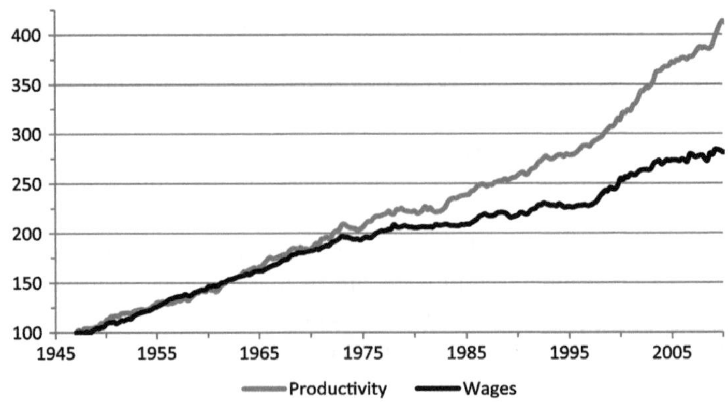

Fig. 3.2 Productivity and real wages in USA

Table 3.1 Growth in Productivity and Real Wages, U.S. 1947–2011

Years		Productivity growth %		Wages growth %		Ratio Annual	Difference Annual (%)
		Total	Annual	Total	Annual		
1947–1970	23	85	2.7	83	2.7	0.98	−0.0
1970–1982	12	19	1.4	14	1.1	0.74	−0.3
1982–2011	29	85	2.2	35	1.0	0.45	−1.2

Note Total refers to the total percent increase during the period. Annual is the annual compounded growth rate. Ratio is the ratio of annual growth rates
Source Susan Fleck, John Glaser, and Shawn Sprague, "The compensation-productivity gap: a visual essay," *Monthly Labor Review*, January 2011: 57–69. Accessed July 21, 2012

hypothesis that wages are equated to the value of marginal product through competition and will as a consequence rise as fast as productivity.

How are wages determined if not by using ME theory? Given the difficulty of ascertaining the marginal product of labor and the uncertainty associated with it, firms satisfice in order to find a viable solution to their problem. They use heuristics and signals to determine the wages of their workers. Of course, education, diploma, work experience, age, gender, ethnicity, and appearance also all play a role. That does not mean that anticipated productivity is not part of the guesstimate, but the above signals are used as proxies or rough gauges of expected productivity. In addition to the above attributes, the history of wages, custom, the degree of unionization, concentration within the industry, the rate of profit of the firm, and the institutional structures in place also matter a lot. While education does play a role in determining wages, it does not explain as much of the differences in income as S&N insinuate. It explains only about 15 % of the variation across occupations.

"While the market can work wonders in producing… goods and services in an efficient manner, there is no invisible hand which ensures that a laissez-faire economy will produce a fair and equitable distribution of income and property" (S&N p. 243). Finally, they admit to an imperfection in market processes, but they fail to suggest remedies to redress this imbalance. What is the sense in producing goods efficiently if the market cannot distribute income efficiently? If it cannot distribute the rewards of production efficiently, it will not produce well-being efficiently.

And why are S&N silent on what a fair distribution of income would be? Rawls suggests that a just distribution is one that we would except in a social contract if we were to design it behind a "veil of ignorance," if we were to be thrown into the society at random, that is to say, if we did not know where in the income distribution we would end up.[16] Choosing behind such a veil, and not knowing any of our future attributes, we would no doubt want to ensure that we would not end up in a disadvantaged position, because for the desperately poor and marginalized in society, life is hardly worth living.

[16] John Rawls, 1971. *A Theory of Justice*, Harvard University Press.

The gist of Rawls' argument is that if you would not dare to enter a society at random, then that society must not be a good one. Our choices after we know our social position will be biased if we have a privileged position because no one likes to give up advantages. Yet, we do not deserve to be born into a rich or a poor family, to be born with certain talents, or smarter or better looking than average because these are just a matter of luck or arbitrary allocation. Hence, it can hardly be fair for the fruits of these attributes to accrue to us personally. In other words, the assignment of property rights in these attributes is arbitrary as they are based on luck and rewards ought not to be based on them. Justice, he argues, cannot depend on a lottery. Hence, Rawls suggests that we should maximize the welfare of the least advantaged in the society, insofar as that is the system risk averse individuals would choose behind a veil of ignorance. S&N desperately want to live in an efficient society, but I doubt seriously whether they would be willing to enter this society before they knew there IQ. Most others would like to live in a decent society. Choosing between efficiency and justice, I, and most of my students queried, would prefer the latter.

"With advancing technology and improved capital goods, American workers enjoy higher wages while working fewer hours. These are the fruits of long-term economic growth" (S&N p. 249). They have a good imagination. The hours worked data in Figure 13-1 is misleading as it fails to report that it pertains to both part-time and full-time workers and many of their part-time workers work fewer hours not by choice but because they are not allowed to work full time. The average full-time worker is working 42.6 hours a week just 0.9 hour less than in 1994 when data began to be collected on this variable; moreover, the average of full-time and part-time workers together is still 39 hour, not very different than it was in the 1970s.[17] And 26 % of the labor force is working more than 41 hours per week.[18] In the manufacturing sector by itself, workers have been working about 40 hours a week as far back as 1946.[19] Actually, I suspect that these are the official working hours reported and many of the overtime spent on the job by salaried employees are not accounted for in these statistics.

Actually, many people have been working more toward the end of the twentieth century in order to keep up with the Joneses.[20] It is also noteworthy that there are more persons working per family today than in prior decades as the labor force participation

[17]Bureau of Labor Statistics, "Average Hours, Persons Who Usually Work Full Time, All Industries," http://beta.bls.gov/dataViewer/view/timeseries/LNS12505054 accessed March 25, 2015. Bureau of Labor Statistics, "Seasonally adjusted hours series from the Current Population Survey," http://www.bls.gov/opub/ils/pdf/opbils84.pdf accessed October 5, 2014.

[18]Bureau of Labor Statistics, "Persons at work in agriculture and nonagricultural industries by hours of work" http://www.bls.gov/cps/lfcharacteristics.htm#hours accessed October 5, 2014.

[19]St. Louis Fed, "Average Hours of Work Per Week, Production Workers, Manufacturing, Total for United States," http://research.stlouisfed.org/fred2/series/M0829BUSM065NNBR accessed October 5, 2014.

[20]Frank, R.H. (1999). *Luxury Fever: Why Money Fails to Satisfy in an Era of Excess*. New York, Free Press.

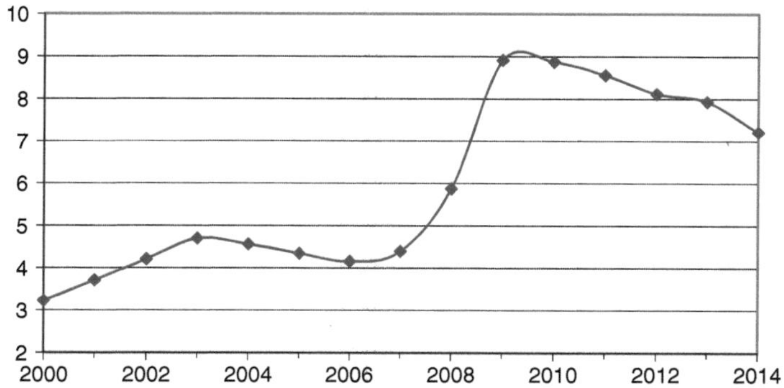

Fig. 3.3 Number of part-time workers unable to work full time

rate of women has increased markedly. "The combined weekly work hours of dual-earner couples with children… has increased by an average of 10 hours per week from 81 to 91 hours."[21] Thus, households have been supplying more work rather than less and still have a very hard time making ends meet (Fig. 3.3).

S&N's wage data are also bad for many reasons, but one is that it includes also the mega-salaries of CEOs and other top managers and averages are influenced disproportionately by these super-salaries. So the $30 per hour indicated in their graph (p. 349) is way off. The average hourly wage among full-time workers (including salary employees) is actually $22 per hour, while the median is at $17.50.[22] The mean for part-time workers, however, is merely $11.8 per hour well below a middle-class wage.[23] In addition, 25 % of the labor force earns $11 or less and 10 % earns 8.24 or less.[24] Among part-time workers, 25 % earn $7.5 or less per hour.[25]

In other words, the evidence points to a much more pessimistic view of wage trends than S&N's imagination conjures up. Actually, men's wages have been stagnating since 1968[26] (Fig. 3.4), and median household income in 2013 was

---

[21]"Sloan Work and Family Research Network Fact Sheet," http://wfnetwork.bc.edu/pdfs/overwork.pdf accessed October 5, 2010.

[22]U.S. Department of Labor. National Compensation Survey: Occupational Earnings in the United States, 2008. U.S. Department of Labor. http://www.bls.gov/ncs/ocs/sp/nctb0717.pdf accessed October 5, 2014.

[23]U.S. Department of Labor. "Full-time and part-time workers: Mean hourly earnings for major occupational groups," http://www.bls.gov/ncs/ocs/sp/nctb0716.pdf accessed October 5, 2014.

[24]U.S. Department of Labor. "Civilian Workers, Hourly wage Percentiles," http://www.bls.gov/ncs/ocs/sp/nctb0729.pdf accessed October 5, 2014.

[25]U.S. Department of Labor. "Part-time civilian workers: Hourly wage percentiles" http://www.bls.gov/ncs/ocs/sp/nctb0731.pdf accessed October 5, 2014.

[26]United States Census, The 2012 Statistical Abstract "Median Income of People With Income in Constant (2009) Dollars by Sex, Race, and Hispanic Origin" http://www.census.gov/compendia/statab/cats/income_expenditures_poverty_wealth/income_for_persons.html accessed October 5, 2014.

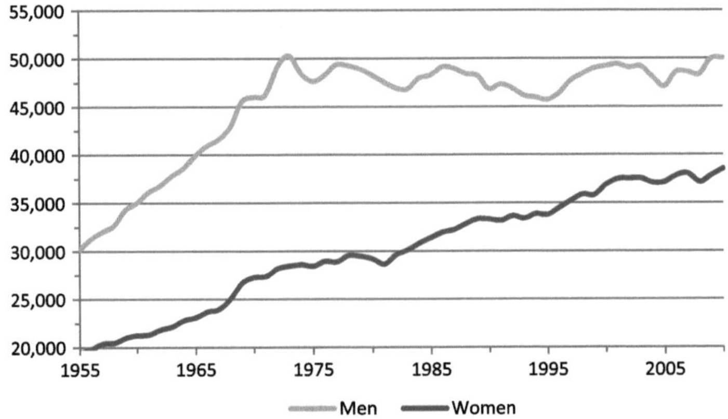

Fig. 3.4 Median income of full-time year-round workers by gender in 2010 dollars

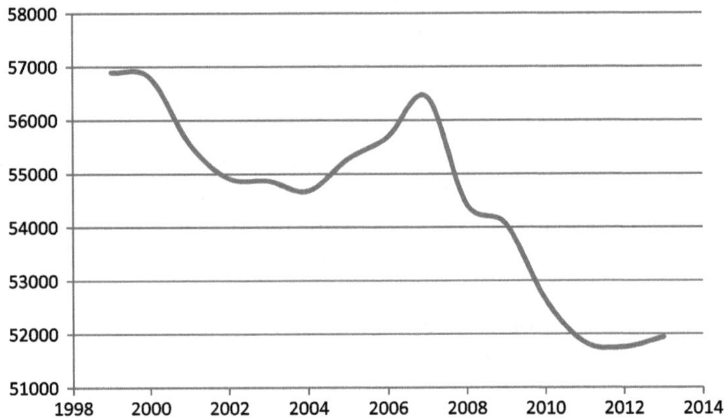

Fig. 3.5 Real median household income in 2013 dollars

$5000 (or 9.5 %) less than in 1999 and at the level of 24 years earlier.[27] Such declines in household income have not occurred for an extended period of time since the Great Depression. In sum, a more accurate view of the labor market points to the harsh reality facing American families today. This is particularly true of minorities, those without a college education, and new entrants into the labor market (Fig. 3.5). For example, the underemployment rate among African Americans is 21 %!

"the demand for a factor of production reflects the marginal productivity of that input" (S&N p. 249). "Reflects" is an ambiguous word and again unscientific.

[27]St. Louis Federal Reserve, "Real Median Household Income in the United States," http://research.stlouisfed.org/fred2/series/MEHOINUSA672N accessed October 5, 2014.

After all, there are distorted reflections. Does it mean that wage equals the value of marginal product or that there is some unspecified relationship between the two variables? In any event, only in a perfectly competitive factor market—and these do not exist in the real world—would their statement be at all relevant. Regrettably, they fail to point out that this result does not hold in presence of endemic underemployment as we have today. In that case, wage is depressed to close to subsistence regardless of the productivity of labor.

The statement is also patently false for occupations in which there is an artificial shortage such as for medical doctors on account of the successful efforts of the AMA to limit the number of practicing physicians. They can extract a monopoly price for their services. It also does not hold for occupations in which productivity is impossible to measure such as for teachers or firemen. In short, their "law" is practically useless for the most important segment of the economy, namely the labor market.

"most Americans work between 35 and 40 hours a week, without much leeway to increase or cut back their weekly hours" (S&N p. 251). It is worth pointing out that a large number of workers feel overworked.[28] Among male managers and professionals, average hours worked in the 1980s and 1990s increased from 44.0 to 45.1 hours per week and the share working more than 49 hours a week increased from 31 to 38 %.[29] Managers and professionals are still clocking in at 43 hours a week. It is well known that people are living more harried lives than ever before. Families with two workers have increased their labor input by 10 hours within a generation at the end of the twentieth century from 81 to 91.[30] And Americans work an amazing 400 hours more per annum than most of their West European counterparts even though their income is higher.[31]

"wage rates differ enormously" (S&N p. 251). Of course, but the crucial question is how much of the difference is justifiable? According to a careful study, some 40 % of wages in the finance sector are actually rents, i.e., that much above a comparable employee in another sector and the extraordinary salaries in that sector can be linked to the era of deregulation beginning in the 1980s (Fig. 3.6).[32] The laxity of corporate governance also means that CEOs can extract an enormous share of profits for themselves and for upper management, and therefore, their salaries are

---

[28]Juliet Schor, *The Overworked American: The unexpected decline of leisure*. Basic Books 1993.

[29]U.S. Department of Labor. Bureau of Labor Statistics. "Are Managers and Professionals Really Working More? Issues in Labor Statistics." Summary 00-12, May 2000. http://www.bls.gov/opub/btn/archive/are-managers-and-professionals-really-working-more-pdf.pdf accessed October 8, 2014.

[30]Sloan Network (2008). Questions and answers about overwork: A Sloan Work and Family Research Network fact sheet. Chestnut Hill, MA: Boston College. http://wfnetwork.bc.edu/topic.php?id=12 accessed October 8, 2014.

[31]Organization for Economic Cooperation and Development, "OECD Statistical Extracts," http://stats.oecd.org/Index.aspx?DataSetCode=ANHRS accessed October 8, 2014.

[32]Thomas Philippon and Ariell Reshef, 2008. Wages and Human Capital in the U.S. Financial Industry: 1909–2006, www.nber.org/papers/w14644 accessed October 8, 2014.

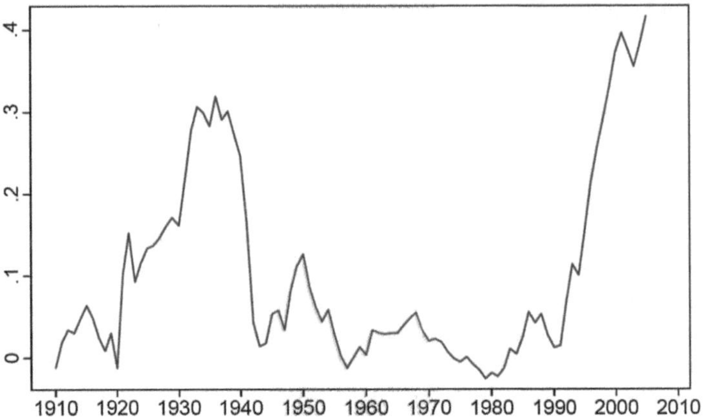

Fig. 3.6 Excess wages in the financial sector

completely disconnected from realism and reflect more their monopoly position within the organization.

"Part of the high salaries of these professionals should be viewed as a return on their investment in human capital-a return on the education that makes these highly trained workers a very special kind of labor" (S&N p. 255). Note again this strange formulation: "should be viewed." Is some authority saying that we should view them as such even if they are not? Are the salaries a return to education or are they not? And how much of the high salaries is a return on their investment? This is another unscientific statement.

It is worth pointing out that a considerable part of those high salaries is a return to the inborn talent or genetic endowment of those professionals for which they did not do anything, and for which, according to Rawls, they do not deserve to receive compensation. That part of their salary is pure rent, i.e., an unjustified reward for their luck and is unrelated, in the main, to investments or to their merit.

"The 'winners' in athletics, entertainment, and finance far outdistance the runners-up in the race for compensation. Top entertainers or athletes can now give a single performance that reaches a billion people via television and recordings…" (S&N p. 256) exactly. That is the nature of a winner-take-all economy.[33] The real question is whether such system of rewards is fair. Note that in the sports sector, the high salaries are due to the institutional structure of the industry, namely the fact that sports are exempt from antitrust regulation and as a consequence operate as a cartel. No wonder that those employed in the sector earn monopoly wages. Shaquille O'Neil would not be earning $20 million a year if the NBA were not exempt from the antitrust laws and be an effective cartel. It is a mistake to allow sports to profit from their privileged position, i.e., from the fact that they are protected from competition. Moreover, such super-salaries would also

[33]Robert Frank and Philip Cook, 1995. *The Winner-Take-All-Society* (New York: The Free Press).

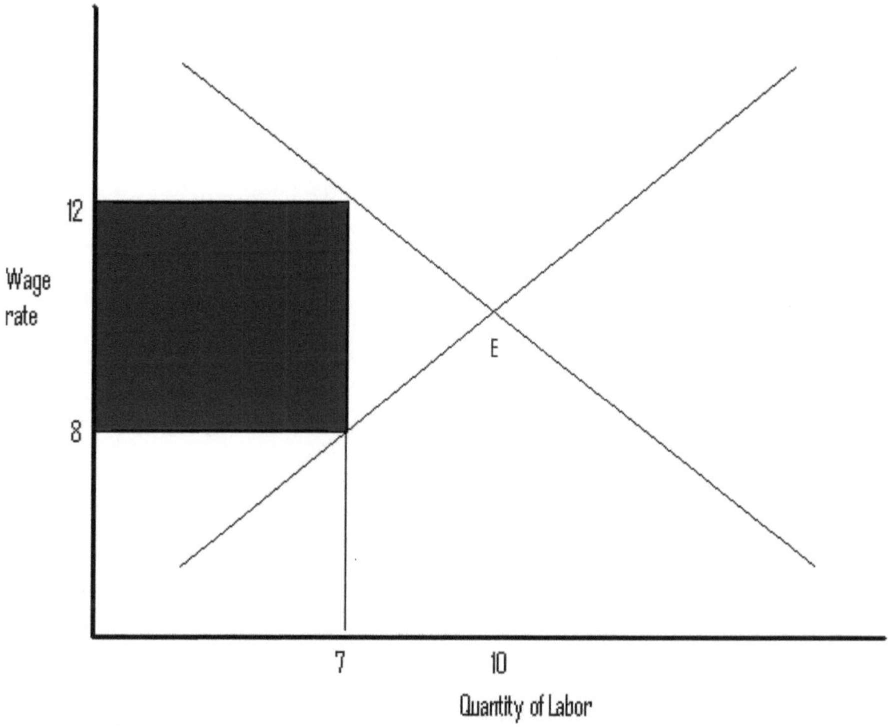

Fig. 3.7 Unions capture a part of the rents earned by oligopolies

not be earned if the team had to pay for using the Internet, created at society's expense. The same, of course, applies to the billionaires of finance. The Internet also helps them and they earn astronomical salaries because of the institutional structure including corporate governance and government support including lax oversight.

Unemployment caused by labor unions (S&N p. 259). This is blackboard economics at its best, but S&N forget to provide evidence and to mention that their discussion and their diagram 13–6 refer to a perfectly competitive firm. However, unions have not been active in perfectly competitive industries. Rather, they have been most active in the public sector and in sectors which are oligopolies and are therefore earning profits. Thus, the aim of unions is to obtain a share of the profits for the employees in which case they do not create unemployment at all but merely transfer income from the wealthy to the poor (Fig. 3.7).

The firm depicted in Fig. 3.7 is ***not*** producing in a perfectly competitive market in which the number of workers hired would be 10. Instead, it is producing with fewer workers (7) because the firm has demand for its products that it can produce with 7 workers. It is thus producing fewer goods, hires fewer workers, and charges a higher price than a perfectly competitive firm would. Workers receive a wage of

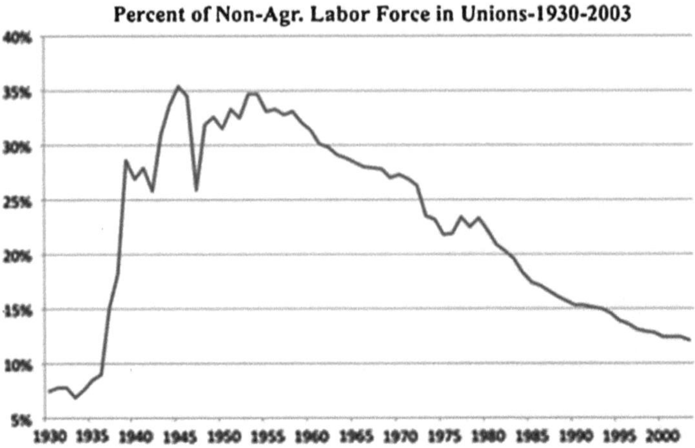

Fig. 3.8 Share of labor force in unions

$8 per hour, the least amount at which they are willing to work. But their marginal product ($12) is greater than their wage. The difference of $4 per hour accrues to the profit of the firm (assuming no fixed cost for the sake of simplicity). So the role of the union is to extract a bit of this excess profit. Note that in this case, the firm continues to produce with 7 workers as long as the workers do not demand an increase greater than $4 which it is not likely. So the increased wage does not bring about any layoffs, but profits do decrease. Now that is not so bad for an economy with as much inequality as in the USA. Unions merely redistributes income from profits to wages.

"if unions succeed in raising their wages above competitive levels, their gains come at the expense of wages of nonunion workers. This analysis is supported by empirical evidence showing that the share of national income going to labor has changed little over the last six decades" (S&N p. 260). This assertion is outdated. Labor's share has been declining from a peak of 68 % of national income in 1970 when unions were much stronger than they are today to 62 % in 2011 when unions are weaker and a negligible factor in the labor market (Figs. 3.8 and 3.9).[34] So the decline in labor unions certainly did not bring about an increase in employment and labor obtained a smaller share of national income.

However, these data are biased because the share of national income going to labor includes the billions earned by CEOs. These mega-salaries of super-managers are considered labor income from the statistical point of view. Thus, labor is not used here in the classical sense of workers, and the true labor income would be even lower. Furthermore, it is very odd that per capita income of men have been

[34]These numbers include compensation including health benefits and pension payments. The wage share alone has been declining by even more—from 58 to 50 %. Jared Bernstein, "Why Labor's Share of Income is Falling," *The New York Times*, September 9, 2013.

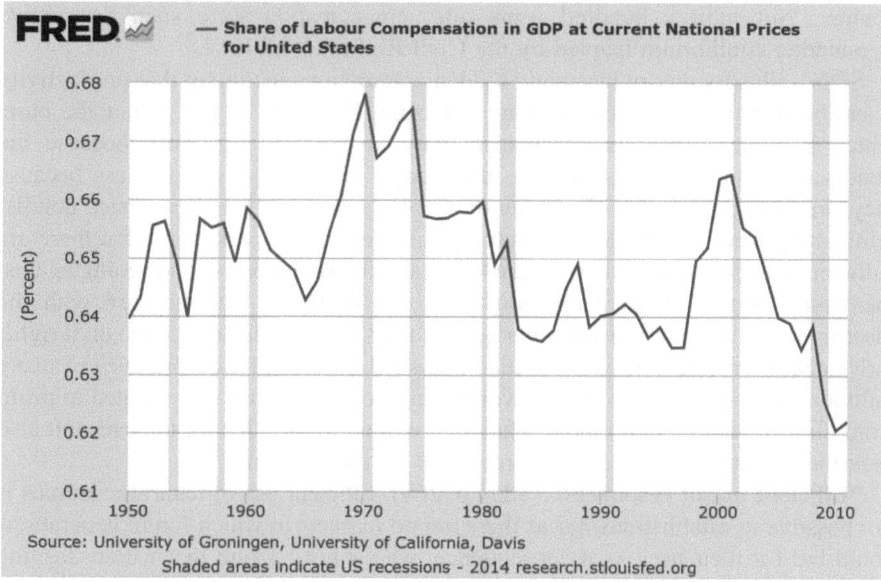

Fig. 3.9 Labor's share in gross domestic product

stagnating throughout the last quarter of the twentieth century just as labor union membership was declining (Fig. 3.4). If labor unions had depressed the wages of the rest of the labor force, one would expect that salaries would increase with the decline in labor unions. Of course, that was not at all the case for men. I infer that income of men has been stagnating, because the weakness of labor unions enabled management to obtain a bigger share of profits. Union membership was still about 21 million in 1981 but is 12.4 million today.[35] The lack of countervailing power enabled corporations to depress wages without increasing employment.

Discrimination is self-correcting because **"Nondiscriminating firms could enter the market, undercut the costs and prices of the discriminating firms by hiring mainly brown-eyed workers, and drive the discriminating firms out of business"** (S&N p. 262). Only "Alice-in-Wonderland" economists would make such an absurd claim. We know that discrimination was not self-correcting but had to be defeated with blood and iron as S&N mention two pages later. "Alice-in-Wonderland" economics becomes morally moribund when one considers how utterly destructive and demeaning discrimination is and what it does to the soul of someone refused service at Woolworth's lunch counter in Greensboro, NC. Just ask Joseph McNeil, Franklin McCain, Ezell Blair, Jr., and David Richmond who started a sit in 1960, because they were not served a cup of coffee at a white-only

[35]US Bureau of Labor Statistics, "Union affiliation of employed wage and salary workers by selected characteristics" http://www.bls.gov/cps/cpslutabs.htm accessed October 8, 2014.

counter. Not until a hundred years after emancipation were such destructive free-market equilibrium banned by the Civil Right Act of 1964.[36]

S&N's illusory theory has many hidden assumptions including that productivity is easily ascertainable prior to hiring someone. However, if that is not the case, which is always, then the mechanism they invoke will not work because the nondiscriminating firm will assume that people willing to work for less because they are less productive. Furthermore, it also assumes that there exist nondiscriminating firms which have enough capital to enter the market and that there are sufficient numbers of people who can withstand the social pressure of going against the cultural norm of discrimination. This was definitely not the case with the discrimination against African Americans in the USA. The history of the civil rights movement is replete with self-sacrifice that shed blood and took the lives of many individuals. These rights were not won through entrepreneurs who wanted to profit from discrimination but by those who were willing to sacrifice for the cause. It also took the power of the state to enforce these rights with guns.[37]

"Efficient use of resources" (S&N p. 269). Efficient use of natural resources is not possible to establish insofar as there are no markets in which future generations could bid for their use. As a consequence, we cannot be sure that we are leaving sufficient resources for the use of generations yet unborn. However, we could establish an institution of ombudsman who would advocate on behalf of future generations. That might help the situation at least to some degree.

"When property rights are well defined…negotiation can sometimes operate to produce an efficient resolution in the presence of externalities" (S&N p. 278). This statement is again ambiguous because it fails to specify the conditions which lead to an inefficient resolution of the problem. However, they should have mentioned that it does make a difference how the property rights are initially allocated, because of the endowment effect. The endowment effect implies that giving up a right is psychologically more discomforting than gaining the right which is comforting.[38] Those who hold the right to pollute would require more compensation to stop polluting than he/she would be willing to pay to obtain the right to pollute. Hence, negotiations favor the status quo.

"An efficient strategy for containing climate change requires weighing the marginal costs of reducing carbon-dioxide (CO_2) emissions against the marginal benefits" (S&N p. 278). Unfortunately, we do not know the potential damage with certainty since we do not know the full extent of the harm that is being caused by such phenomenon as the extinction of species whose monetary value is

---

[36]Wikipedia contributors, "Greensboro sit-ins," http://en.wikipedia.org/wiki/Greensboro_sit-ins accessed October 8, 2014.

[37]Youtube video, "Little Rock Nine," http://www.youtube.com/watch?v=K1pVN111QsY accessed October 8, 2014. Youtube video, "Little Rock High School," http://www.youtube.com/watch?v=6UhvIO6cKLk accessed October 8, 2014.

[38]Daniel Kahneman, Jack Knetsch and Richard Thaler, 2000. Anomalies: The Endowment Effect, Loss Aversion, and Status Quo Bias. In Daniel Kahneman and Amos Tversky (eds.), 2000. Choices, Values, and Frames. Cambridge University Press, pp. 159–170.

impossible to ascertain. Moreover, we need to consider the costs that will fall on future generations which are also impossible to ascertain. Hence, an efficient solution is beyond our reach, but I would prefer a fail-safe strategy to one that tries to guess at such calculation. Would we want to take even one in a million chance on possibly pursuing a policy that might be irreversible and after we are long gone, perhaps a couple of hundred years from now might lead to the extinction of our own specie?[39]

Global warming has begun to have ominous consequences. For instance, the sea level has risen in Norfolk, Virginia, by a threatening 14.5 inches causing tidal flooding. So the city is now spending 1.25 million on a short stretch to help protect just one neighborhood.[40] They have to bear the cost that was not caused by them. That is the reality of a negative externality.

"We can identify innovational profits... as the temporary excess return to innovators and entrepreneurs. These profit earnings are temporary and are soon competed away by rivals and imitators" (S&N p. 297) this is the way things work only in Alice-in-Wonderland economics. The profits are permanent, because due to barriers to entry they are not competed away. Some examples in 2010 in billions of dollars are as follows: Microsoft: 15, Wal-Mart: 14, Exxon: 19, Chevron 10, Conoco: 5, Goldman Sachs 13, J.P. Morgan Chase 12, Wells Fargo 12, Bank of America 6, Apple 6, Coca Cola 7, just to name a few major corporations.[41] These profits are not being competed away because of government-granted patents and because corporations do not sit still to wait until competitors impact their profit margins, but they continually change their products so that they can avoid a perfectly competitive solution in the long run. Corporate Business profits tripled since 1998 to reach $1.8 trillion by 2013, at a time when median household incomes have fallen by $5000 or by 9.6 %. That is a great divergence between profits and incomes. There is nothing temporary about that. S&N continue to make claims without presenting any evidence.

---

[39]Natural Resource Defense Council, "The Cost of Climate Change," http://www.nrdc.org/globalwarming/cost/contents.asp accessed October 8, 2014.

[40]Leslie Kaufman, "Front-Line City in Virginia Tackles Rise in Sea" *The New York Times*, November 25, 2010, http://www.nytimes.com/2010/11/26/science/earth/26norfolk.html?_r=1&nl=todaysheadlines&emc=a2 accessed October 8, 2014.

[41]St. Louis Federal Reserve. "Corporate business: Profits before tax," http://research.stlouisfed.org/fred2/series/A446RC1A027NBEA "Real Median Hourhold Income in the United States" http://research.stlouisfed.org/fred2/series/MEHOINUSA672N accessed October 8, 2010.

Chapter 4
Applications of Economic Principles

"Within high-income countries, no simple law relating tax burdens and the citizenry's well-being can do justice to the true diversity of the fiscal facts of nations" (S&N p. 305). Actually, there are a couple of patterns worth a mention. One is that Anglo-Saxon countries and their overseas offshoots tend to tax less and that is particularly true for the USA. This phenomenon is based on a deeply rooted anti-government culture. The other is that the countries in the New World were founded by immigrants who were self-sufficient and did not want to rely on the community and that spirit has been propagated from generation to generation and even amplified with the Reagan presidency. Americans want minimum government even if they are worse off for it. They think they can spend their money more wisely than the government can but that turns out to be falsified by the evidence. The happiest people live in high-tax countries in Scandinavia; the happiest people in the world live in Denmark. The Western and Northern European model of the welfare state has high taxes but also provides numerous services for which Americans have to pay inflated prices, such as health care and education. In these countries, 100 % of the population has health insurance and university education has only a nominal tuition or is completely free as in Germany. They also enjoy life longer, spend half of what we do on education and health care (that includes taxes paid toward these services), live safer with less crime, much less stressed, and are less indebted, and the typical college graduate leaves university with zero debt in contrast to the typical US college graduate who leaves with an indebtedness of $25,000. Maybe higher taxes are not such a bad option as they are made out to be.

Of course, the taxpayers have to pay for these services; nonetheless, there are considerable advantages to have the government sponsor them. The advantages include economies of scale including ease of administration in contrast to the thousands of insurance companies in the USA and equally importantly, the government uses its power to bargain vis-a-vis doctors, hospitals, and the pharma industry. So the government has a much better control over healthcare expenditures. No wonder that Europeans pay half of what Americans pay for health care and still

© The Author(s) 2016

J. Komlos, *Principles of Economics for a Post-Meltdown World*,
SpringerBriefs in Economics, DOI 10.1007/978-3-319-27828-5_4

live one or two years longer. So their government is much more efficient at providing health care than the free-market version in the USA.

European governments are also in a position to curtail the cost of higher education, so in the end, it costs the taxpayers about half as much as the privately organized counterpart in the USA. In America, college tuition has exploded between 1978 and 2014 rising by as much as 6 % per annum during the mid-1980s. Supply of private colleges and universities has not decreased, so it must be demand that was driving the tuition increases. That is not surprising in a tight labor market in which prestigious institutions hold the ticket to a decreasing number of high-paying jobs. The elite schools take advantage of their monopoly position extract as much of the future salaries of the students as the market will bear. No wonder that real prices tripled in the intervening 36 years.[1] There is nothing like that in Europe. In fact, there is no other country in the world that puts so much financial burden on students (and their parents) as the USA does. In the meanwhile, total student debt has ballooned to one trillion dollars.[2] And there is no other country in the world in which college presidents earn million dollar salaries. So the citizens of high-tax countries reap a myriad of advantages. And because university admission is not dependent on the income of the parents, poor students have a better chance of social mobility than in the USA. No wonder Western Europeans live more satisfied lives.

Four functions of the government (S&N p. 306). This list leaves out many important functions such as consumer protection, national defense, providing for future generations, regulating economic activity, environmental policy, enforcing contracts, rebalancing income inequality, and making sure that the balance of power is maintained in the economy, i.e., that no one group obtains an inordinate share of economic power. The balance of power is crucial for the maintenance of democratic political structure, because otherwise the political system can easily morph into an oligarchy. Actually, many observers including MIT economist Simon Johnson have noted that our system has already morphed into an oligarchy.[3]

"Early capitalism was prone to financial panics and bouts of inflation and depression" (S&N p. 308). Late capitalism is also prone to financial panics as we just experienced in 2008. The depression of 1929–41 was also not an example of early capitalism but of well-developed capitalism. In other words, S&N bend over backwards not to admit that instability is inherent to the free-market system and

[1]College Board, "Tuition and Fee and Room and Board Charges over Time, 1973–74 through 2013–14, Selected Years," http://trends.collegeboard.org/college-pricing/figures-tables/tuition-and-fee-and-room-and-board-charges-over-time-1973-74-through-2013-14-selected-years, accessed October 9, 2014.

[2]Andrew Martin and Andrew W. Lehren, "A Generation Hobbled by the Soaring Cost of College," *The New York Times*, May 12, 2012 http://www.nytimes.com/2012/05/13/business/student-loans-weighing-down-a-generation-with-heavy-debt.html?pagewanted=all&module=Search&mabReward=relbias%3Ar%2C%7B%222%22%3A%22RI%3A16%22%7D, accessed October 9, 2014.

[3]Simon Johnson, "The Quiet Coup," *The Atlantic*, May 2009. http://www.theatlantic.com/magazine/archive/2009/05/the-quiet-coup/307364/, accessed April 26, 2015.

they have become much more prevalent around the globe as the crisis in Mexico, Argentina, Russia, Thailand, South Korea, and many other countries to indicate. Instability is particularly problematic in the financial system as Hyman Minsky pointed out decades ago.[4] In the Minsky model, the economy is a complex system in which there are debt contracts which commit firms to pay a stream of money from their profits. Those financial commitments are based on expectation of profits which are often overly optimistic and over the business cycle become speculative, and many debt obligations cannot be fulfilled. Bankruptcy follows, and with systemic risks, a snowball effect develops and the whole economy can spin out of control. Instability therefore rises out of the debt economy and its impact on the dynamic behavior of the complex economic system.[5] "The financial instability hypothesis is a model of a capitalist economy which does not rely upon exogenous shocks to generate business cycles…. The hypothesis holds that business cycles of history are compounded out of… the internal dynamics of capitalist economies…"

"Why are there such vast differences in compensation among jobs?" (S&N p. 328). The reasons he cites pertain, in the main, to reasonable differences. However, the astronomical salaries and bonuses are actually rents, that is to say neither earned, nor deserved. It is a matter of being in the right place at the right time and being able to take advantage of profits of corporations by writing one's own checks. How are profits distributed in Goldman Sachs? As far as CEOs like Lloyd Blankfein are concerned, what difference does it make, how much he pays out in bonuses, and how much dividend he pays to shareholders? He probably seeks what seems like a reasonable split between them. There is nothing competitive about the distribution of spoils. Basically, the CEO decides.[6]

Similarly to CEOs, the salary of college presidents has increased extravagantly in tandem with the rise in tuition ***not*** because there has been a decline in the supply of individuals capable of leading such institutions and ***not*** because there has been

---

[4]Hyman Minsky, The Financial Instability Hypothesis, Working Paper No. 74. The Levy Economics Institute of Bard College. http://www.levyinstitute.org/, accessed October 9, 2014.

[5]In Minsky's words: "the greater the weight of speculative and Ponzi finance, the greater the likelihood that the economy is a deviation amplifying system. The first theorem of the financial instability hypothesis is that the economy has financing regimes under which it is stable, and financing regimes in which it is unstable. The second theorem of the financial instability hypothesis is that over periods of prolonged prosperity, the economy transits from financial relations that make for a stable system to financial relations that make for an unstable system.

In particular, over a protracted period of good times, capitalist economies tend to move from a financial structure dominated by hedge finance units to a structure in which there is large weight to units engaged in speculative and Ponzi finance." In case of contractionary monetary policy, the net worth of firms "will quickly evaporate. Consequently, units with cash flow shortfalls will be forced to try to make position by selling out position. This is likely to lead to a collapse of asset values." Hyman Minsky, The Financial Instability Hypothesis, Working Paper No. 74. The Levy Economics Institute of Bard College. http://www.levyinstitute.org/, accessed October 9, 2014.

[6]Marianne Bertrand and Sendhil Mullainathan, 2001. "Are CEOs Rewarded for Luck? The Ones Without Principals are," *The Quarterly Journal of Economics*, 116, 3:901–932; Jerry W. Kim, Bruce Kogut, and Jae-Suk Yang, 2015. "Executive Compensation, Fat Cats, and Best Athletes," American Sociological Review 80, 2:299–328.

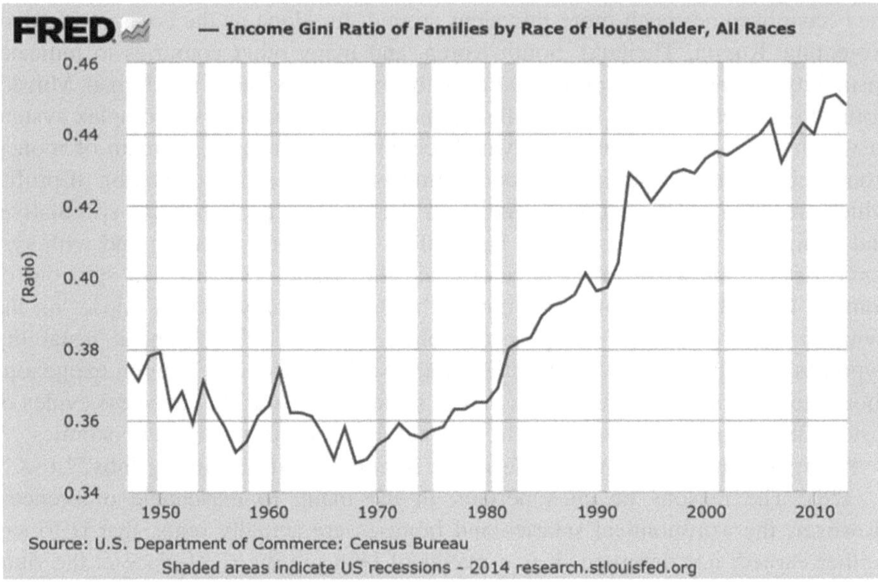

Fig. 4.1 Trend in the Gini coefficient, 1947–2013

an increase in demand for such people as there is but one president per college. Rather, the presidents of these organizations have been able to capture a larger share of the rents that were being generated on account of the increase in tuition.[7] In 2011, there were already 42 presidents earning in excess of million dollars, obviously not a competitive salary.

"Inequality fell over most of the twentieth century and then began to rise around 1970" (S&N p. 329). Inequality began to fall after the stock market crash of 1929 and began to increase after 1968 but in 1980 was still only at the level of 1952. Between 1970 and 1980, the Gini coefficient—a measure of inequality—increased at a rate of 0.5 % per annum, whereas in the subsequent two Republican administrations, the rate accelerated to 0.9 % per annum (an increase of some 82 %) (Fig. 4.1).[8] As with so many other adverse developments, the turning point was actually not 1970 but 1980 with Ronald Reagan's insistence on deregulation, lowering taxes on the wealthy, his message of disparaging government, and pro-business world view. Thus, these changes in inequality did not just happen as implied by S&N's statement and were not brought about by market forces alone but

[7]Tamar Lewin, "Pay for U.S. College Presidents Continues to Grow," December 15, 2013 http://www.nytimes.com/2013/12/16/us/pay-for-us-college-presidents-continues-to-grow.html?module=Search&mabReward=relbias%3Ar%2C%7B%222%22%3A%22RI%3A16%22%7D, accessed October 19, 2014.

[8]St. Louis Federal Reserve, "Income Gini Ratio of Families," http://research.stlouisfed.org/fred2/series/GINIALLRF, accessed October 10, 2014.

by Reaganomics and the hammering of the unions which changed the balance of power in favor of those who were already powerful, deregulation which enabled the corporations to outsmart consumers, and the decline in the tax rate for the super-rich which made them richer. Over time, wealth begot wealth and power begot power. This is not supposed to happen in a democracy. But it did happen because a substantial number of people were unable to recognize their own self-interest and voted for people who did not represent their interest. As a consequence, the wealth created by the economy is accruing and most likely will continue to accrue to an increasingly smaller share of the population.

"In taking steps to redistribute income from the rich to the poor, governments may harm economic efficiency and reduce the amount of national income available to distribute" (S&N p. 331). Too bad S&N do not explain why redistribution "may" harm efficiency. What is the evidence and how strong is the evidence? They prefer to remain ambiguous. Maybe they think that rich would work less if their taxes were raised and that would lead to a decline in total income. However, that supposition is not based on empirical evidence. It assumes that incentives are linear to infinity and are absolute and not relative. Maybe they believe that if someone's after-tax salary is $1000 per hour, she will work less than someone who earns $2000 per hour? I have not seen any evidence supporting such claim. Rather, I believe that it would not make any difference whatsoever but rather reduce the number of luxury yachts, the import of designer dresses, and Maseratis. After all, there was no shortage of top managers when the top marginal tax rate was 90 % in the 1950s under the Eisenhower administration. So I think that the reason they do not provide evidence is that the inefficiencies associated with the redistribution are merely illusory and serves the purpose of defending the current lopsided distribution of income.

Would the 403 American billionaires work less if their wealth were halved?[9] Would that money spent on education or health improve human capital sufficiently to foster not only well-being but economic growth as well. In short, such a redistribution is much more likely to improve the efficiency of the economy. It is precisely for this reason that the Western European economies have done quite well: Social spending on health care, education, and other public goods actually fosters rather than inhibits growth.[10]

Besides, absolute incomes are not crucial in creating incentives in the stratosphere income group. Rather, relative incomes matter. The literature on measuring life satisfaction suggests that the welfare effects of an increase in income are minimal in the long run as long as everyone's income increases as well. An increase in income increases life satisfaction only if mean income remains unchanged. In other words, the rank order counts and not the absolute level of incomes in

---

[9]Together their wealth adds up to $1.3 trillion. http://www.forbes.com/2010/03/09/united-states-richest-people-warren-buffett-michael-bloomberg-billionaires-2010-gates_slide.html, accessed October 9, 2014.

[10]Peter Lindert, 2004. *Growing Public: Volume 1, The Story: Social Spending and Economic Growth since the Eighteenth Century.* Cambridge University Press.

increasing life satisfaction and motivating people. That is precisely why we are not more satisfied with our lives now than we were fifty years ago. If the model propagated by S&N—that our welfare is directly related to income—were true, then people today would be much more happier than in the past. In fact, they would be euphoric, insofar as we are immensely wealthier. The implication of this research is that it is not the magnitude of the top salaries that motivates the super managers but the fact that their salaries are greater than those of the rest of the employees of the firm and at least as great as those of their peers. It is the relative standing that matters and not the absolute magnitude itself.

So redistribution from the rich to the poor has no incentive effects, but there are many positive effects of a safety net provided by the redistribution of the Western and Northern European welfare states. It provides security, so the citizens feel better, knowing that if unexpected disaster strikes, they have something to fall back on. Moreover, countries with a tighter safety net have lower crime rates. So people are freer to travel at night. They are less anxious about the safety of their children. They have fewer break-ins, less car theft, and so forth. So all in all, they are less stressed out and enjoy a higher quality of life. In other words, a higher level of taxation leads to a more balanced society which in turn leads to a higher welfare on average.

There is yet another aspect to consider. We are not particularly good at allocating our time between work and leisure. The reason is that we expect additional income to improve our lives, so we choose to work instead of taking leisure. But other people will do the same in order to keep up with your level of consumption. The end result is that everyone is working more, but the pecking order remains unchanged, and if one's position in society remains constant, additional income does not produce as much welfare as we expected. So we choose to work more, but our additional income also has negative externalities because it causes other people to work more as well. As any negative externality, this kind of externality too should be taxed so that one imposes less of this externality on others. As a consequence, increased tax on labor income can improve the quality of life as everyone enjoys more leisure, while maintaining the same level of life satisfaction insofar as the social hierarchy remains unchanged.

Later on, S&N contradict their statement above (p. 331) by admitting that the "Empirical evidence, however, suggests that the damage of taxes on work effort is limited… Most studies find that taxes have only a small impact on labor effort for middle-income and high-income workers." What is all the fuss about them?

"Some economic studies indicate that by taxing income rather than consumption, total saving is reduced" (S&N p. 333). Where are these studies? The inconvenient truth is that saving has declined even though disposable income has increased substantially and the tax rate has declined as well (Fig. 4.2). In 1984, the tax rate was 10.4 % and the saving rate 10.7 %, but by 2005 the saving rate declined to 2.5 %, while the tax rate remained relatively unchanged at 9.9 %. Thus, taxes have not had any impact on saving. The correlation coefficient between the two data series depicted in Fig. 4.2 is an insignificant 0.16.

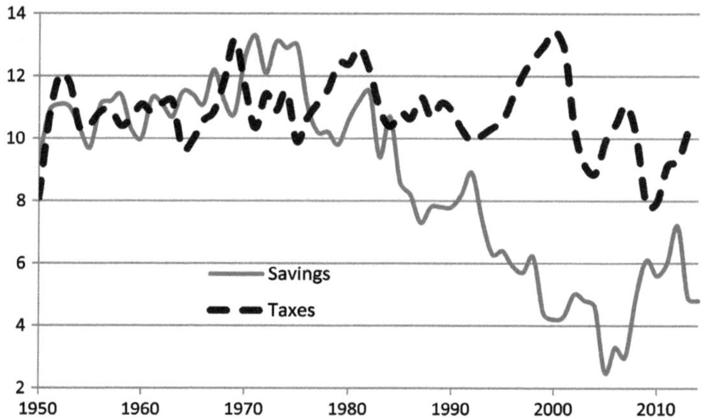

Fig. 4.2 Personal savings and taxes as a percentage of personal disposable income

"economists worry that the nation's saving rate has declined sharply because of generous social programs-especially social security and Medicare-that reduce the need for people to save for old age and health contingencies" (S&N p. 333). Instead of worrying, they should have looked at some data which indicate that the saving rate did not decline at all after the introduction of social security in 1935 or with that of Medicare in 1965. Instead, it increased from 4.7 % in 1929 and reached a maximum of 13 % from 1971 to 1975 and did not begin its steep decline until 1986.[11]

Is it a coincidence that this was just the moment when inequality began to increase? I should think not. With income inequality increasing, it appears quite plausible that the middle class did not want to fall behind the consumption of the wealthy and was able to keep up with the Jones's only by dipping into its saving rate. Moreover, is it a mere coincidence that it was in the 1980s that the first generation reached adulthood who was weaned on the bombardment of consume-now messages of the TV age? The corporations won: There was no profit to be had from consumers saving. There was no advertisement for saving and that is how this became the instant gratification generation. Social security and Medicare are just a scapegoat.

In any event, social security is anything but generous. It basically provides a poverty-level safety net for the elderly. Medicare, too, does not pay for everything and does not pay 100 % of even eligible treatments. So it is by no means large enough to reduce the rate of saving.

"Egalitarian countries like Sweden and the Netherlands, which provided cradle-to-grave protection for their citizens, found declining labor-force participation, growing unemployment and rising budget deficits" (S&N p. 333).

[11] http://www.census.gov/compendia/statab/cats/income_expenditures_poverty_wealth.html, accessed October 9, 2014.

They have good imaginations! The inconvenient truth is that this is just ain't so. Sweden and the Netherlands had an unemployment rate in September 2010 of 7.8 and 4.4 % compared to USA's 9.6 %.[12] In 2014, the unemployment rate in Sweden was 7.9 and 4.4 % in the Netherlands and 6.2 % in the USA.[13] So the unemployment rate was consistently lower in the Netherlands and sometimes lower sometimes higher in Sweden. At the same time, the USA has a much higher underemployment rate than those two countries.

The labor force participation rate was 65 % in Sweden, 64.8 % in the Netherlands, and 63.7 % in the USA in 2012.[14] Not much difference there either. The budget deficit was 0.3 % of GDP in Sweden, 3.3 % in the Netherlands, and 7.6 % in the USA.[15] However, the European welfare states offer immense advantages. Their citizens enjoyed 100 % health insurance coverage which enabled them to live 1–2 years longer than do people in the USA and a relative child poverty rate of 5–7 % compared to the USA's 22 %.[16] Moreover, the cost of college education is born by the community so that a college graduate does not start working life with a substantial debt of $26,000 as they do in the USA.

"The principle of comparative advantage holds that each country will benefit if it specializes in the production and export of those goods that it can produce at relatively high cost" (S&N p. 342). Unfortunately, they fail to delineate the conditions under which the theorem holds and conditions under which it does not hold. Instead, they make it sound as though it were universal such as the law of gravity. Well, it isn't! Super-honest economics would call this a theorem about barter between two countries and not trade in the modern sense of involving money. As it stands, the discussion is misleading, because it does not hold if trade causes unemployment or if trade deficits are endemic. Hence, it is not applicable to the USA insofar as four decades of trade deficits has damaged the economic fabric substantially.

The deficit increased most rapidly in the last decade: from $100 billion to $800 billion in 2006.[17] Just think of the effect of drawing so many billions worth of purchasing power out of the economy year after year and stimulating the rest of the world's economy! No wonder that we have such a high level of underemployment! And no wonder that the capacity utilization of our factories is under 80 %.[18] Warren

---

[12] http://stats.oecd.org/index.aspx?queryid=251, accessed October 9, 2014.

[13] http://research.stlouisfed.org/fred2/series/LRHUTTTTSEA156N; http://research.stlouisfed.org/fred2/series/NLDURHARMADSMEI; http://research.stlouisfed.org/fred2/series/UNRATE/downloaddata, accessed April 30, 2015.

[14] http://research.stlouisfed.org/fred2/series/SWELFPRNA; http://research.stlouisfed.org/fred2/series/NLDLFPRNA; http://research.stlouisfed.org/fred2/series/CIVPART, accessed April 30, 2015.

[15] http://research.stlouisfed.org/fred2/series/CASHBLSEA188A; http://research.stlouisfed.org/fred2/series/CASHBLNLA188A; http://research.stlouisfed.org/fred2/series/CASHBLUSA188A, accessed April 30, 2015.

[16] www.unicef.org/media/files/ChildPovertyReport.pdf, accessed October 9, 2014.

[17] http://research.stlouisfed.org/fred2/series/BPBLTT01USA636S, accessed April 30, 2015.

[18] http://www.federalreserve.gov/releases/g17/, accessed October 9, 2014.

Buffett warned that "The U.S. trade deficit is a bigger threat to the domestic economy than either the federal budget deficit or consumer debt and could lead to political turmoil… Right now, the rest of the world owns $3 trillion more of us than we own of them."[19] The riot in Baltimore at the end of April 2015 is just one manifestation of the frustration that builds up when manufacturing jobs are exported and underemployment brings about a sense of hopelessness in a substantial segment of the population.

In 2014, US exports of goods and services were $2.3 trillion, while imports amounted to $2.9 trillion, implying that the deficit was no less than 0.6 trillion dollars.[20] The deficit with China alone was $342 billion—more than half of the total.[21] During the last two decades, USA's trade deficit added up to no less than a $10 trillion stimulus package for the rest of the world. That is like spending 12 times as much as the "Obama stimulus" of 2009 except it was spent not at home but abroad. At a time when the USA does not have nearly enough jobs for its own citizens, it is foolhardy to be offshoring so many jobs.

With trade deficits, our living standards will decline eventually. Instead of buying consumer goods which depreciate quickly, the Chinese have been buying firms such as Smithfield Foods for $4.7 billion and real estates like the 99-year lease on Waldorf-Astoria for $2 billion. That implies that US income in the future will be lower as the profits of these enterprises will be going into their bank accounts and that of US residents.

So trade is not always mutually beneficial. As a matter of fact, on p. 398 S&N indicate that our trade deficit subtracted $708 billion from GDP in 2007. In other words, GDP could have been 5 % higher if our trade would have been balanced. That would have reduced unemployment. Using the rule of thumb that $1 million worth of exports creates about 5 jobs in the USA, the elimination of the $600 billion deficit of 2014 would have created some 3 million jobs, thereby reducing the unemployment rate by a third.

"As European clothing penetrates the American market, American clothiers will find prices falling and profits shrinking, and they will begin to shut down their factories… America as a whole benefits…" (S&N p. 343). But that statement assumes that the workers who are displaced from their jobs in the contracting sectors will find employment in the expanding ones. But those assumptions are not at all valid today: Displaced North Carolina textile workers do not have the credentials to work in the expanding IT sector or on Wall Street or as health professionals. And when trade leads to unemployment, the theory of comparative advantage no longer works as assumed and both sides no longer benefit.

---

[19]Buffett has proposed import certificates as a way to make sure that trade is balanced. http://www.berkshirehathaway.com/letters/growing.pdf, accessed October 9, 2014. U.S. Liabilities to foreigners at the end of 2010 is at $4.3 trillion. http://www.federalreserve.gov/econresdata/releases/intlsumm/usliabforinst20101130.htm, accessed October 9, 2014.

[20]http://www.bea.gov/iTable/iTable.cfm?ReqID=9&step=1#reqid=9&step=3&isuri=1&903=128, accessed April 30, 2015.

[21]https://www.census.gov/foreign-trade/balance/c5700.html#2014, accessed April 30, 2015.

To be sure, some people will benefit, while others will lose their livelihood. The crucial issue is if such a policy—that helps some at the expense of others—is at all ethical? The answer is obviously no, as the policy would not be Pareto optimal unless the gainers were to compensate the losers. But that is never the case: The losers are never made whole. We do not have the right to enrich some at the expense of others. Only once we realize that and act upon that, will we be able to create a humanistic economy.

There is yet another problem: What does it mean that "America as a whole benefits." How do they aggregate the gains and losses? I thought that S&N claimed earlier in their text that utility levels were not comparable. But now they do compare welfare of the losers and gainers nonetheless and without blinking an eyelash. How deceptive! Suppose a worker gets laid off and loses $50,000. Suppose also that 90,000 people gain $1 each by purchasing a product that is now imported and is cheaper. S&N add this up and obtain a net gain for America of some $40,000. However, notice that there are crucial assumptions behind such a clandestine arithmetic. The impact on the welfare or utility of these two groups of people is not really comparable. The worker who loses his/her job is devastated if he/she cannot find another job and that has been the standard among low-skilled workers of late. In contrast, the group that gains may not even notice the $1 gain to their welfare. So their utility will increase infinitesimally, meaning that it is asymptotically zero and 90,000 times zero is still very close to zero.[22] The end result is a substantial decline in welfare of one person and no real change in the welfare of the others in this example. So one can get very different results from the ones advocated by S&N.

In short, the crass simplification overlooks the main social, political, and ethical problems of coping with the effects of factory shutdowns as a consequence of trade liberalization. Theorems that work on the blackboard fail miserably on Main Street. Humanistic economics would prescribe not only that "America as a whole" benefit, but that everyone in America benefits or at least not be made worse off. S&N acknowledge some of these problems on p. 349, but then why state the theorem unconditionally to begin with?

The American workers gain 20 %, while the European workers gain 5 % (S&N p. 343–44). Humanistic economists would consider such lopsided distribution of the gains from trade as unfair.

"As far as a single country is concerned, all the other nations can be lumped together into one group as "the rest of the world"" (S&N p. 348). Hmm. Not if they have different exchange rate regimes and different comparative advantages and produce very different goods. That is like adding oranges and apples. How do you lump France and Haiti together? Not so easy to do as they make it out to be.

Triangular trade (S&N p. 348). It is easy to imagine this working if all the countries are producing only one good because then there is no competition among

[22]Suppose their income is $50,000 per capita. Then, their gain is effectively 1/50,000 or something like 0.00002.

the countries. With two goods in each country some of which compete with one another, there can be losers, indeed. Why is it that so many countries have practically nothing to offer in international trade?

"Economists generally believe that free trade promotes a mutually beneficial division of labor among nations; free and open trade allows each nation to expand its production and consumption possibilities, raising the world's living standard" (S&N p. 349). The crucial question is not what economists believe but what the facts are. It is noteworthy that few countries benefited greatly from free trade outside of the European countries and their overseas offshoots. The industrial revolution occurred a quarter millennium ago, and yet most countries have not been able to keep up with the core countries. The few who have, like China, Japan, South Korea, Taiwan, and Singapore, did it by managing trade. They certainly did not let free trade rule their economies.

Infant industries particularly need to be protected and fostered. Here is how it works. Suppose computers have just been invented in country A and a firm can produce them for $100 dollars in year 0. As it starts building them, it accumulates knowledge about how to do it better and cheaper—called learning by doing—and in the following year can build it for $95. Now firms in country B see the opportunity but do not have the inside knowledge, so they have to start the process from the beginning as a high cost producer at $100. In other words, they are only going to be able to compete if the government gives them a $5 subsidy or levies a tariff of $5 on computers. First mover advantage means that follower countries have to play catch-up and free trade does not work to their advantage at all. After singing the praises of free trade, S&N (p. 358) finally give short shrift to the infant industry argument just as the Chinese wind turbine manufacturers are penetrating the US market to the detriment of the fledgling home industry.[23]

"Notwithstanding its limitations, the theory of comparative advantage is one of the deepest truths in all of economics. Nations that disregard comparative advantage pay a heavy price in terms of their living standards and economic growth" (S&N p. 349). Big words again: "deepest truths." Rather than being a "deep truth," it is a highly ideological proposition and far from truth as such. It confuses short-term advantage for long-term gain. It overlooks the many examples which demonstrate how countries benefited in the long run from protection from foreign competition. It is noteworthy, for example, that two industrial powerhouses of the twentieth century, the USA and Germany, both had substantial protective tariffs in the nineteenth century in order to enable their industries to get off the ground and become powerhouses. Otherwise, they would have had a very difficult time to compete with England, the forerunner of industrialization in the nineteenth century. There must be something wrong with the argument which is not backed by historical evidence.

[23]"We cannot sit idly by while China races to the forefront of clean energy production at the expense of U.S. manufacturing," Senator Sherrod Brown, an Ohio Democrat, said. http://www.nytimes.com/2010/12/16/business/global/16wind.html?_r=1&hp, accessed October 9, 2014.

The actual deep truth is that no country developed into an economic heavyweight by practicing free trade. None, not even England! It gained competitive advantage over the Dutch in the seventeenth century not through free trade, but by the mercantilist protection of its Navigation Acts which prohibited the use of foreign ships for trade between it and its colonies which earned it a lot of profits. Finally, on p. 360 S&N present evidence that USA historically was a high-tariff nation. I guess they have no problem with contradicting their earlier contentions.

"Who decided that we would import just this amount of clothing…? A Chinese planning agency? … No, the amount of trade was determined by supply and demand" (S&N p. 351). By singing the praises of supply and demand they skirt, the more interesting question would be, however, who is going to find work for the unemployed textile workers? Can the labor market provide them with the new skills they need, provide them with moving expenses so they can relocate where there are jobs at their skill level, and make sure that they have jobs in the end? It is a very doubtful proposition. In fact, the real world has not conformed to their theory.

"The overall social impact [of the tariff] is,… a gain to producers of $250, a gain to government of $200, and a loss to consumers of $550. The net social cost (counting each of these dollars equally) is therefore $100" (S&N p. 353). But should one count these dollars equally? In the earlier section of the text, the argument was that utility is not comparable between people, but here suddenly, the off-the-cuff assumption is made that a dollar is valued equally by everyone concerned. Instead, the most commonsense assumption is that the utility generated by a dollar gained by a producer millionaire is not the same as, in fact, it is much less than the utility lost by the worker who loses the equivalent dollar but who is far from being a millionaire and instead is living from hand to mouth from day to day. A dollar is simply not valued equally by the two.

The second hidden problem with their accounting is that the consumers do not really lose $550 but $350 because the government does not swallow the tariffs but provides $200 worth of services to the consumers. Actually, they might well provide a lot more than $200 worth of services to consumers if they invest the amount into basic research or education that pays handsome returns.

Their third clandestine assumption is that all the workers who find work in the expanding textile sector were fully employed prior to the imposition of the tariff. However, this is not a relevant scenario at a time when 15 % of the labor force is un (der)employed and factories are operating at 75 % capacity. This is particularly the case as it ought to be clear that going forward underemployment is going to be with us for the foreseeable future. Moreover, the motivation for introducing the tariff is to provide work for the unemployed in the first place. So let us do the arithmetic with the more plausible assumption that the workers had been unemployed before the introduction of the tariff (Fig. 4.3). In that case, the area $B + E = \$50 + \$200 = \$250$ becomes the resources used to produce the textiles and is a gain to the workers provided we overlook the cost of raw materials for the moment. The loss to the consumers is still $A + B + D = \$350$. In addition, the producers also increase their profits by area $A = \$250$. So all of a sudden the gains become $250 + $250 = $500, and the net gain becomes $500 − $350 = $150. In short, once one corrects their accounting for the

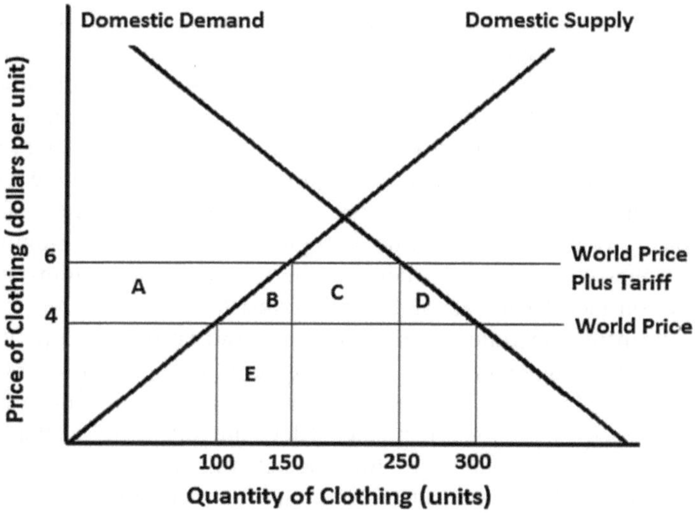

Fig. 4.3 The effect of a tariff on the production, consumption, and import of clothing

hidden and inadequate assumptions, a loss turns into a gain and the tariff suddenly makes a great deal of sense from the society's point of view: It puts people back to work.

"…the nation is wasting resources in textiles" (S&N p. 355). The unemployed workers are also a wasted resource and one that is very costly not only in economic terms but also in social and psychological ones. The deteriorating urban infrastructure in places like Detroit, Milwaukee, or Baltimore and the riots in the latter bears witness to what happens if jobs are exported overseas.

"These workers, materials, and capital would be more productively used in other sectors- perhaps in aircraft or financial services or internet commerce" (S&N p. 355). Has anyone seen an ex-textile worker on Wall Street selling securities? Or in Silicon Valley working for a dot-com firm? Has anyone seen a textile factory moving to Seattle to work on aircraft design?

"Consumers, of course, pay for this protection of the textile industry with higher prices" (S&N p. 355). While they pay a few more dollars for clothing, it is a small part of their budget and a tiny increase in their well-being. It may even be so small that it may not even register. In contrast, for those working in the industry, the existence of their jobs is a matter of their livelihood and a matter of their existence and would make a massive impact on their welfare. Can one weigh the immense suffering of a few against the trivial gains of the many? Why should one put consumers ahead of workers?

"Consumers are induced to cut back on their clothing purchases, channeling funds into food, transportation, and recreation, whose relative prices are lowered by the tariffs" (S&N p. 355). Who knows, perhaps they would also save more for their retirement and feel better about their future or perhaps spend more leisure time with their families and enjoy life more. It would not be so bad to decrease clothing consumption.

"France argued that its citizens need to be protected from 'uncivilized' American movies" (S&N p. 355). I find it rather cynical and overbearing to put the matter in these terms. I do not think that the French put it this way, but rather they chose not to want to become American in spirit, in attitude, and in mentality. I do think it is legitimate to want to maintain one's cultural identity and fend off attempts to undermine it. That is a critical issue with globalization, namely simply put that American businesses and products come at the price of local customs and values which many consider degenerate and therefore resist.

"The mercantilist argument confuses means and ends" (S&N p. 355). S&N confuse short-term temporary gains with long-term strategic ones. Their biased presentation is a reflection of the immense ideological commitment to free trade. However, evidence is not on their side. There are plenty of examples which demonstrate that countries that control trade do better in the long run. I already cited Germany and the USA in the nineteenth century, but even England in the seventeenth century practiced mercantilism before it became economically strong enough to practice free trade. China became a global manufacturing powerhouse by controlling its imports and currency. There are no examples in which free trade helped an underdeveloped economy. Only with oversight were developing countries able to catch up to the West.

"Accumulating gold or other monies will not improve a country's living standard" (S&N p. 355). This is a rather myopic view as current so-called living standards are not the only thing to worry about. Is the future worth thinking about? A current account surplus would surely give a country a sense of security for the longer run, knowing that there are some reserves to commit to future purchases of capital goods, for instance, as new technologies come on board. Savings would also make it possible for the country to withstand a run on its currency as happens time and again, for example, to the peso in 1994 or Thai bhat in 1997. In such crisis situation, reserves are crucial in keeping the country from going into bankruptcy. That is one of the reasons why the Bank of China has a hoard of $4 trillion in cash. They learned their lesson from the Asian financial crisis of 1997.

"why do the proponents of protectionism continue to wield such a disproportionate influence on legislatures?" (S&N p. 355) Where? Certainly not in the USA which is basically a major proponent of free trade. A hundred years from now, most economists will realize that one of the reasons for the decline in American political, military, and economic power was the free trade policies. Following the S&N's principles, it preferred short-term gains for long-term advantage. That is exactly what happened to Great Britain during the late nineteenth and early twentieth centuries when they declined in relatively to its rivals while practicing free trade.

"The reason American workers have higher wages is that they are on average more productive" (S&N p. 356). On average is not at issue. At issue are the unskilled workers who are at risk of foreign competition. Their wage is measured in monetary terms so reflect the prices of the goods they produce. Most unskilled workers are not more productive at all in real terms. That is the problem that leads to their underemployment.

"If America has a comparative disadvantage in industries like textiles or toys, and these industries are intensive in unskilled labor, reducing trade barriers will tend to reduce the wages of unskilled labor in America" (S&N p. 356). It will do more than "tend to reduce" unskilled wages. It will actually equalize wages, or as that is not possible in our case, as American workers would starve on Chinese wages, the jobs will be simply eliminated. That is what has been happening and that is what is meant by exporting jobs. That is precisely why we still have 17 million underemployed workers suffering because of Chinese competition.

"There may also be temporary effects on workers whose wages drop while they look for alternative jobs" (S&N p. 356). What right do S&N have to advocate policies that reduce the welfare of some workers? That is certainly not in the spirit of being a Pareto optimal policy insofar as they are making some people worse off.[24] This is inconsistent after they have touted Pareto efficiency in earlier segment of their text. Furthermore, the temporary became permanent as alternatives did not materialize for so many millions of low-skilled American workers.

"Over the long run, labor markets will reallocate workers from declining to advancing industries, but the transition may be costly for many people" (S&N p. 356). This is the cruel version of capitalism as it imposes the costs of free trade on poor workers in order to benefit those who are already better off. If the reallocation works at all, it works only in the long run through the generations as older workers die off and younger workers are allocated to the new sectors. It does not work well for the uneducated and unskilled. Humanistic economics would advocate full compensation to the workers who lose income, so they would not have to bear the burden of free trade policies.

"The cheap-foreign-labor argument is flawed because it ignores the theory of comparative advantage" (S&N p. 356). In this Pollyanna economics, the theory of comparative advantage remains a theory without empirical foundations. It surprisingly ignores the complications of unemployment, the role of profits, as well as strategic trade policy including the effect on infant industries. Insofar as it ignores money, it is, in fact, not even a theory of trade but a theory of barter. So a super-honest economics would not even call it trade but barter. Hence, the theory of comparative advantage is one of the most misleading ideologically tainted contentions of mainstream economics. Actually, it is cruel as well because it ignores the plight of the displaced workers who become unemployed. But S&N argue in this section that it is ok to injure people as long as it benefits others.

"less productive industries are actually being killed off by the competition of more productive domestic industries. This sounds ruthless indeed"[25] (S&N p. 357). Humanistic economists would not use such "brutal" language. No talk about Pareto optimality here. No mention if the pain of the losers is greater than the

---

[24]See the discussion on their p. 160.

[25]Not clear to me if they mean the competition of more productive foreign industries?

gain of the gainers. I guess they think it is acceptable to hurt people. No wonder that so many people are dissatisfied with their lives in the USA.

A policy of optimal tariffs would not be warranted because"that would be a 'beggar-thy-neighbor' policy… [and] other countries are likely to react" (S&N p. 358). However, Warren Buffett suggested ways to eliminate our trade deficit in such a way that foreigners are not able to retaliate.[26] They ignore such possibilities completely.

"By the appropriate use of monetary and fiscal policy, a country can increase output and lower unemployment" (S&N p. 359). Yeah, we see how effective these policies are today.

"the use of general macroeconomic policies will allow workers displaced from low-productivity jobs in industries losing their comparative advantage to move to high-productivity jobs in industries enjoying a comparative advantage" (S&N p. 359). They keep on repeating this maxim. I guess they believe that repetition will make it sound truer but it does not. Perhaps they just want to brainwash the reader. I do not know of or heard of displaced manufacturing workers getting work in the expanding IT branch. A few examples would have been useful. You know, like Joe, the textile worker landed a job as a janitor on Wall Street or something like that. There were 2.3 million people in 2009 who were unemployed for longer than a year. I guess that must seem more than temporary for them.[27]

From 1991 to 1999, the United States created 16 million net new jobs while … its trade deficit increased sharply… (S&N p. 359). To invoke such, simple correlation is not a very sophisticated argument. The number of unemployed still fluctuated between 5.9 and 9.6 million people in the 1990s.[28] That is hardly trivial even by today's standards when the number of un(der)employed is closer to 17.0 million. There was not a causal relationship between job creation and the trade deficit. Of course, it is altogether possible that new jobs will be created during a period when the trade deficit increases, but the good times of the 1990s was based on the dot-com bubble and unstable finance. The point is that that there was easy Chinese money in the 1990s that kept on fueling the economy, while the American consumer was getting deeper in debt by using their wealth as ATM machines. In 1990, household debt in the USA amounted to about 83 % of income, but by the end of the decade, it was closer to 92 %. The boom was sustained, in other words, in spite of the trade deficit by borrowed funds. In 2007, indebtedness was even higher at 130 %. That gives one an idea of how precarious our situation is and how misleading the idea of free trade at any cost is. But indebtedness is not a part of S&N's theory of chalkboard economics.

[26]Buffett has proposed import certificates as a way to make sure that trade is balanced. http://www.berkshirehathaway.com/letters/growing.pdf, accessed October 9, 2014. U.S.

[27]ftp.bls.gov/pub/special.requests/lf/aat30.txt, accessed October 9, 2014. The front page of the Wall Street Journal (2/3/09) reported "Gloomy Prospects: People began lining up Saturday to apply for Miami firefighter jobs." There were thousands in the crowd for the 35 openings.

[28]ftp.bls.gov/pub/special.requests/lf/aat1.txt, accessed October 9, 2014.

We are still paying the interest on these deficits and will for a long time to come. No wonder that our standard of living is declining. Jeffrey Sachs put it this way: "The late 1990s are often regarded as the halcyon days of the policy regime, with their rapid growth, low inflation, and high employment. In retrospect, however, we also see in these years the collapse of private saving, the explosion of foreign borrowing, the Dot.com bubble, the start of the housing bubble, and the failure to address underlying structural problems."[29]

"This [infant industry] argument must be weighed cautiously" (S&N p. 359). Note that there was no caution in their voice when they were talking about "killing" industries. They proudly declared that to be a matter of progress. Now all of a sudden they prefer a cautious tone even though the protection of infant industries is an important policy instrument for developing countries to catch up to their more developed counterparts.

"Tariffs and import protection are an inefficient way to create jobs or to lower unemployment" (S&N p. 359). However, they might be the only way to save jobs and not to increase unemployment. And why don't they present some evidence that they are inefficient? And are there better ways to create jobs?

[29]Jeffrey Sachs: Rethinking Macroeconomics. *Capitalism and Society*, Vol. 4 [2009], Iss. 3, Art. 3. http://www.bepress.com/cas/vol4/iss3/art3, accessed October 9, 2014.

Chapter 5
Macroeconomics: Economic Growth and Business Cycles

"Japan…was unable to shake off high unemployment… after 1990" (S&N p. 369). I do not know where they get their numbers from, but Japan's unemployment rate was between 2 and 5 % after 1990. In 2015, their unemployment rate is 3.6 % about 2 % less than in the USA.[1] Per capita gross national income peaked in 1996.[2]

"Key factors in long-term economic growth" (S&N p. 369). The key factors differ if one is among the leading rich countries or among the followers. The followers had a very difficult time catching up without state support. In fact, all of the follower countries that were able to approach Western levels of income had governments which supplemented the free market with industrial policy. The free market is pretty bad at setting long-range goals. And the long run is not merely a series of short runs in case of playing catch-up with the advanced countries. All countries with high growth rates such as China or those that caught up with the West, such as the Four Asian Tigers, Taiwan, Singapore, Hong Kong, and South Korea as well as Japan, had some government involvement in setting economic goals and oversight. Such policies included state-controlled low-interest rates for exporting industries or Japan's fostering strategic industries and allowing monopolies to develop and funneling capital to major industries and import controls. The free market played a secondary role in setting strategies of catching up with the West.

Goals of macroeconomic policy (S&N p. 370). Note that many important goals are missing from this list. Such overlooked goals include a high quality of life, reduction of inequality, low level of environmental degradation, sustainable development, reduction of uncertainty, low-level volatility, providing public goods, maintaining the stability of the financial system, and intergenerational justice. These would be advocated by humanistic macroeconomists.

---

[1]http://stats.oecd.org/index.aspx?queryid=451.

[2]http://www.stat.go.jp/english/data/chouki/; http://data.worldbank.org/indicator/NY.GNP.PCAP.CD?page=2.

© The Author(s) 2016

J. Komlos, *Principles of Economics for a Post-Meltdown World*,
SpringerBriefs in Economics, DOI 10.1007/978-3-319-27828-5_5

"As foreign investment in the nation increased, the United States by 2008 owed on balance around $2½ trillion to foreigners" (S&N p. 376). They have the causation backward. The USA became indebted to foreigners not because foreigners wanted to invest in the USA but because the Chinese earned a lot of cash on the cheap goods they sent to the US. In other words, the earnings on the exports to the USA preceded the investments. One might also mention that by 2014 the debt owed to foreigners increased to $6 trillion with an interest payment of some $150 billion which is about half of all taxes paid by corporations in the USA.[3] That is about twice as much as the federal government spends on education.[4] In other words, it is a substantial sum that leads to a decline in the US standard of living. This is precisely the scenario I referred to in the previous chapter to counter the idea that comparative advantage leads to a rise in the standard of living if there is a deficit.

"Aggregate demand is affected by the prices at which the goods are offered, ..." (S&N p. 376). However, it also depends on what Keynes called "animal spirits," that is to say by consumer confidence and expectations of future prices. "Even apart from the instability due to speculation, there is the instability due to the characteristic of human nature that a large proportion of our… activities depend on spontaneous optimism… Most, probably,… our decisions to do something…, [are] the result of animal spirits—a spontaneous urge to action rather than inaction…."[5] In other words, S&N are misleading in depicting demand as a stable function of prices. Demand is far from being stable as the Great Recession has amply demonstrated.[6] Consumer confidence can vary by a lot and is at historical lows right now (Fig. 5.1). Ask Richard Wagoner CEO of General Motors at the time when the government had to bail it out before it went bankrupt. He knows about it. After all, the index has been compiled since World War II.[7] I am surprised that S&N "forgot" to mention it. The demand for big ticket items such as automobiles and houses can be very volatile and does not depend just on prices (Fig. 5.2). The demand for automobiles went from 4.5 million units to 1.1 million units in 1932, but even in "normal" times, demand can fluctuate a lot: from 7.9 million units in 1955 to 4.5 million units in 1958.

In post-Meltdown economics, we also have to pay more attention to credit conditions and the rate at which consumers are able to borrow. Alan Greenspan's easy-money policies led not only to the double bubbles of the turn of the twenty-first century, but it also led to people using their housing wealth as ATM machines which in turn fueled consumption.

---

[3]https://en.wikipedia.org/wiki/National_debt_of_the_United_States#Foreign_holdings.

[4]http://www2.ed.gov/about/overview/budget/budget16/summary/16summary.pdf p. 3.

[5]John M. Keynes, *The General Theory of Employment, Interest and Money*, London: Macmillan, 1936, pp. 161–162.

[6]George A. Akerlof and Robert J. Shiller, *Animal Spirits: How Human Psychology Drives the Economy, and Why It Matters for Global Capitalism*, Princeton University Press, 2009.

[7]http://en.wikipedia.org/wiki/University_of_Michigan_Consumer_Sentiment_Index.

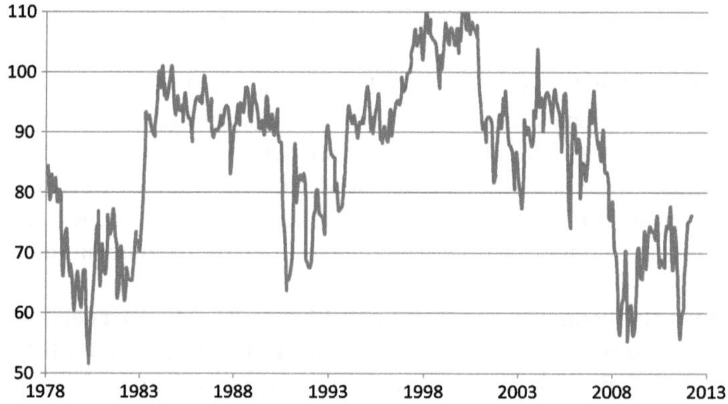

Fig. 5.1 Consumer confidence index

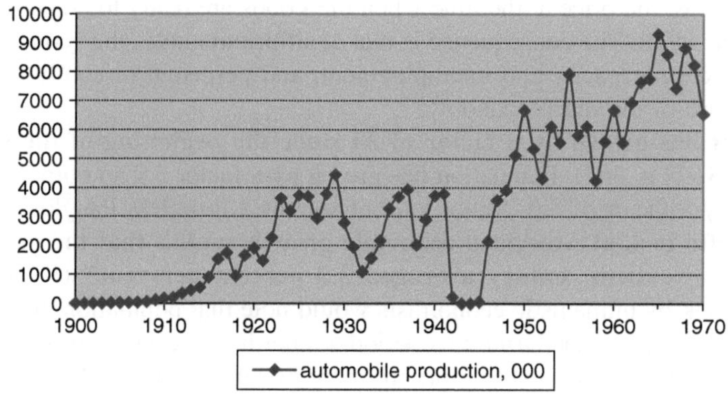

Fig. 5.2 Automobiles produced in the USA

Aggregate demand and Aggregate Supply discussion (S&N p. 376) leaves out inventories held by businesses. Insofar as suppliers do not produce on order, they have to forecast the quantities demanded and are not able to produce exactly as much as consumers want. More often than not they err on the side of overproduction. As a consequence, the difference between the quantity demanded (AD) and the quantity supplied (AS) is absorbed in inventory. So it would be better to say that $AD = AS - \Delta I$ where ΔI is the increase in inventory.

"Taxation subtracts from incomes, reduces private spending, and affects private saving. In addition it affects investment and potential output" (S&N p. 376). Why do they have to put taxation in such a negative light? Taxation is also used to pay for transfer payments in which case it does not detract from private spending. It pays for essential services such as that of policemen and teachers. It pays for investments in infrastructure such as harbors and roads without which the economy would be in bad shape. It was the government who paid for research that led to the Internet, and rocket science that made satellite communication possible. And these paid handsome returns. So it does not subtract at all; it adds a lot.

"Monetary policy" (S&N p. 376) leaves out the banking sector. It is the banking sector that creates most of the money stock through their loan policies.

Figure 19.5 (S&N p. 378) leaves out the financial sector entirely. This is why so many economists were baffled by the Great Meltdown. Bubbles were not supposed to happen. They are not used to thinking of banking and credit and leveraging in the context of macroeconomics. It is very strange to think of macroeconomics without a financial sector.

"How does the economy reach its equilibrium?... A macroeconomic equilibrium is a combination of overall price and quantity at which all buyers and sellers are satisfied with their overall purchases, sales, and prices" (S&N p. 379). Would be nice, if we could have such a blissful situation where everyone was satisfied, but reaching equilibrium is by no means as simple as S&N argue. Producers see the current price, but production is not instantaneous so that they have to forecast the price at the time when the goods are ready to be shipped. That is not simple at all. The consequence is that equilibrium eludes the economy. There is always excess capacity and unemployment, and perpetual disequilibrium is the salient feature of the macroeconomy.

"Output has grown by a factor of 34 since the beginning of the twentieth century" (S&N p. 381). Population has grown by a factor 3.9 so output per capita increased by a factor of 8.6. Still a lot, but sounds a little less Panglossian.

"A careful look at American economic growth reveals that the growth rate during the twentieth century averaged 3.3 percent per year" (S&N p. 381). A careful look by humanistic economists would note that population grew at a rate of about 1.25 % per year during this period so that in per capita terms output grew by 2 % per annum. This is still a lot, but more down to earth. Perhaps they would then not refer to it later on the page as "the tremendous rise in output." Notice also that they fail to mention the tremendous maldistribution of the benefits of growth.

"Many economists believe that the measure growth understates true growth because our official statistics tend to miss the contribution to living standards from new products and improvements in product quality" (S&N p. 381). Many economists are wrong because they overlook the many negative externalities that are not subtracted from GDP and therefore make GDP biased upward by a lot. For example, it completely overlooks the value of environmental degradation like the oil damage done by the Gulf oil spill. The rockets fired at Baghdad as a part of the "shock and awe" strategy ended up increasing GDP as the military no doubt ordered replacements, but did it improve living standards? Fully 1/3 of US households were victims of some crime in 2010.[8] You have to ask yourself why it is the case that societies with less income inequality have less crime. In short, most

[8]http://www.gallup.com/poll/145205/New-High-Households-Report-Computer-Crimes.aspx?utm_source=alert&utm_medium=email&utm_campaign=syndication&utm_content=morelink&utm_term=Politics.

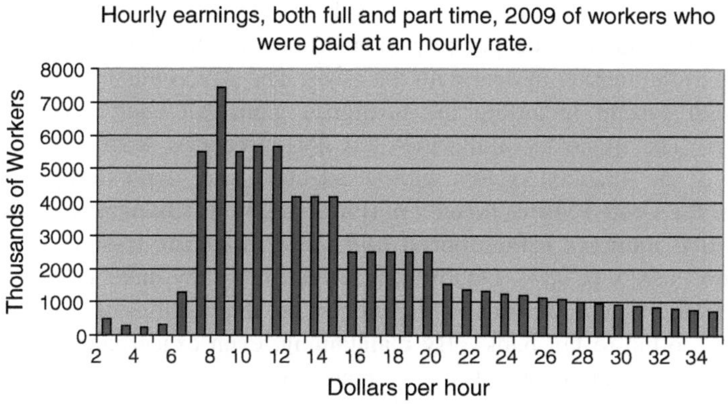

Fig. 5.3 Distribution of hourly wage of part-time and full-time workers

humanistic economists believe that there are dozens of reasons why GDP is a misleading and inferior measure of living standards in the first place. It was never intended to be a measure of living standards but of production.[9] I am surprised S&N do not know that.

"...average earnings rose...to over $30 per hour in 2008" (S&N p. 381). This is a made-up statistic to fit their Panglossian view of the economy. The average in 2009 was in reality $22 per hours but that includes CEO pay and it does not include part-time workers so the true average is lower than that.[10] Without managers, the average was $18.30 and median pay for part-time workers was $8.50 in 2007.[11] The mean pay for both full- and part-time workers receiving hourly wages, that is to say excluding those working on a yearly salary such as CEOs, managers, and bankers, was $15.03, and the median was $12.44. The distribution indicates that there were 2.6 million workers earning below the minimum wage and another million at the minimum wage (Fig. 5.3).[12] So the $30 is a fantasy.

"a good appreciation of the role and limitations of monetary and fiscal policy, reduced business-cycle volatility and led to the Great Moderation" (S&N p. 381). The Great Moderation was pronounced prematurely as it culminated in the Great Meltdown, the biggest crisis since the Great Depression, to the dismay of mainstream economists such as Ben Bernanke. It was not supposed to happen so such threats were not included in their models. The US financial system was too "sophisticated" for that. Finally, free marketeers like treasury secretary Hank

---

[9]Joseph E. Stiglitz, Amartya Sen, and Jean-Paul Fitoussi, Mis-Measuring our Lives. Why the GDP Doesn't Add up. New Books, 2010.

[10]http://data.bls.gov/cgi-bin/dsrv also National Compensation Survey: Occupational Earnings in the United States, 2008. U.S. Department of Labor. http://wfnetwork.bc.edu/pdfs/overwork.pdf.

[11]http://www.bls.gov/ncs/ncswage2007.htm.

[12]Current Population Survey, Table A-23. Hourly earnings of employed wage and salary workers1 paid hourly rates by detailed industry and sex, Annual Average 2009.

Paulson, former CEO of the investment bank Goldman Sachs, turned into an economic czar and tried desperately to micromanage the Meltdown. He did not leave it up to the market to deal with the crisis. The government having to prop up the financial system including the insurance giant AIG and two of the three automakers. The monetary authorities did not appreciate sufficiently to inherent instability of the financial system without adequate and vigilante regulation.

"When the United States faced a major shock to its financial system in 2007–2009, central bankers remembered *and understood* the lessons of the Great Depression" (S&N p. 382). Doubtful, however, that they understood the changes that have taken place in the meanwhile such as the implications of the rise of a large number of too-big-to-fail banks. By maintaining, even exacerbating, this structure the Fed, with Ben Bernanke at its helm, created an unsustainable financial sector that many economists think will lead to a "doom loop" and recurring financial instability. Among these are Simon Johnson, Nouriel Roubini, Nassim Taleb, and a host of others. By purchasing 3.7 trillion dollars' worth of toxic assets, an interventionist Fed bailed out Wall Street but neglected Main Street and at the same time introduced so much moral hazard into the system that any of the giant banks can blackmail the taxpayer at any time in the future for further funds. By doing so, the Fed basically broke the logic of the capitalist system leading to general skepticism among the population and to a dysfunctional political system. As the Nobel Prize winning economist, Joseph Stiglitz, argued, they basically socialized losses and privatized gains and allowed bonuses to be paid to those very bankers who bankrupted their firms in the first place. That does not seem to be such a smart policy. It is questionable that such a system can be maintained in the long run under the new unwritten rules of the marketplace. However, with 11 % un(der)employment[13] and 8 million houses foreclosed the Fed and the treasury failed miserably in bailing out Main Street and in their ultimate goal of getting the economy in high gear. What we got is what Paul Krugman calls a "sour economy." And there is no end in sight.

Another major factor overlooked by many is that the economy was fundamentally on an unsustainable path prior to the Great Meltdown. It had immense trade imbalances and immense budget deficits. These two deficits weigh heavily on future growth and living standards. In addition, the economy went from one bubble to another, i.e., from the Dot.com bubble to the housing bubble as a consequence of Greenspan's easy-money policies. As Larry Summers has been pointing out, it has been two decades since the economy grew at a healthy clip without being sustained by bubble finance created by loose monetary policy.

In other words, monetary policy has been bad and fiscal policy was bad as well. As though that were not enough, inequality increased with people attempting desperately to keep up with the Joneses by going into debt. Hence, economic

[13]Counting those who would like to work but have not search during the previous year (6 million) and counting those who are working part-time but would like to work full time as being half underemployed. 6.4 million part-time divided by 2 equals 3.2 million added to the underemployment. With 14.2 million unemployed in 2009 yields a total underemployment of some 22.4 million out of a labor force of 140 million. ftp://ftp.bls.gov/pub/special.requests/lf/aat8.txt.

growth of the last two decades was a mirage sustained by money from the Chinese Politburo and $3.7 million worth of asset purchases by Ben Bernanke. The idea propagated by the members of the Obama administration that we can "grow the economy" by across-the-board tax cuts and a little bit of Keynesian fiscal stimulus rings hollow at best in light of the tremendous imbalances and structural problems of the economy in the early twenty-first century. By not instituting fundamental structural changes that would have redressed the above issues, by failing to invest in education and in infrastructure that were needed for long-run economic growth, and by failing to support "green industries" sufficiently to wean the country from fossil fuels, the economy was condemned to linger as far as the eye can see. So the Fed did learn *some* of the lessons of 1929 but was not able to modify them sufficiently to accommodate policy today's problems. In the end, Ben Bernanke turned out to fight today's battles with yesterday's strategies. All in all the handling of the crisis was inimical to the long-run health of the economy. Gallup reported that in April 2015, 28 % of Americans were satisfied with the way things were going.[14] So the economic policy did not succeed in increasing the feeling of optimism of the population. Satisfaction level was at 60 % at the time of the beginning of George W. Bush's presidency.

I am not alone in these contentions. In an article, Jeffrey Sachs puts the problem similarly. The crisis is a culmination of an extended period of misplaced macroeconomic policies.[15]

> The crash of 2008 exposed deep failures at the core of macroeconomic policymaking … in the United States…. The American purveyors of the ancien régime hope that a few superficial fixes will get us back on our way. This is not to be. Sustained and widespread future prosperity will require basic reforms in global macroeconomic governance and in macroeconomic science… require[ing] new ways of thinking. Yet business as usual could prove calamitous…

[14]http://www.gallup.com/poll/182438/satisfaction-dips-back-below-april.aspx?utm_source=U.S.%20satisfaction&utm_medium=search&utm_campaign=tiles.

[15]Jeffrey Sachs, Rethinking Macroeconomics. *Capitalism and Society*, Vol. 4 [2009]: 3, Art. 3. http://www.bepress.com/cas/vol4/iss3/art3.

Conclusion

One could continue with the deconstruction of S&N's fallacious textbook. but I think by now the reader must have understood that the book is inadequate for students; in fact, it is fundamentally flawed. It is full of inconsistencies and ambiguities and is consistently misleading in such a way so as to sway the student toward believing in the wonders of the free market system. In other words, it is ideologically committed and as almost all of the other Principles of Economics textbooks provide a succor for the benign neglect of the underclass in this country.

In other words, S&N's depiction of the outlines of economics is very far from following Richard Feynman's admonition of bending over backwards so as not to deceive ourselves and, of course, the readers. Instead, S&N's representation of the economy is nothing less than a fantasy world, one that provides a justification for the existing economic order with its abundant injustices including the terrible distribution of income and endemic unemployment and underemployment. They fail terribly to provide an authentic theory that reflects the human condition in its concrete social, cultural, and political setting. Their book is just one example of the poverty of the mainstream economic methodology. They fail to describe flesh and blood individuals struggling to make ends meet but rely basically on a caricature of a one-dimensional economy inhabited by one-dimensional men whose sole purpose in life is to consume and is so smart and so good at it that he is able reach nirvana by optimizing satisfaction.

The fallacies in the book include the omission of crucial topics that are either not mentioned at all or mentioned only in passing. Their neglect can only lead to a distorted view of the economy. These issues include:

- Sigmund Freud and the importance of advertising in influencing our unconscious. Without it one cannot possibly understand the fundamentals of consumerism. After all, a nephew of Freud was the founder of modern marketing techniques in the USA.
- Pavlovian conditioning and the unbridled efforts of businesses to take advantage of our human weaknesses and profit from our inability to withstand their psychological barrage. Their strategic marketing campaigns outsmart us, and we get caught up in the rat race treadmill. Without recognizing this important aspect of the economy students will never ever be able to comprehend how and why we

© The Author(s) 2016

J. Komlos, *Principles of Economics for a Post-Meltdown World*,
SpringerBriefs in Economics, DOI 10.1007/978-3-319-27828-5

have become a consumer society, a society that is focused intensely on consuming rather than on other aspects of life such as virtue, justice, spiritual development, respect for nature, self-realization, or relationships such as friendship and family.

- that people are not able to be rational and are incapable of maximizing their welfare as Daniel Kahneman demonstrated and for which he received the Nobel Prize. Humans are not robots; they have emotion and often use intuition to make a judgment and not our prefrontal cortex. They are incapable of being consistent. We simply did not evolve like that. None of our organs is perfect. Why should our brains be an exception?
- satisficing for which Herbert Simon received the Nobel Prize and which should be the default model of economic choice inasmuch as real human beings as opposed to imaginary supermen and superwomen are incapable of optimizing. Real people with real cognitive limitations strive to arrive at a satisfactory solution to their problem. This is a very different, though more realistic model, than the one proposed by S&N.
- conspicuous consumption in which wealthy spend on outrageously expensive goods in order to flaunt their riches and establish their position in the social pecking order.
- basic needs, i.e., that there are some goods which differ from all other goods in that they sustain life and by virtue of this fact deserve special consideration.
- that relative income matters beyond basic needs and not absolute income. This is an important omission, because without this concept students will never understand why we are so frustrated as a nation in spite of the fact that per capita real GNP has risen by a factor of 3.7 between 1950 and 2014. Just think about that for a minute. With such a tremendous increase in income and productive capacity, one would expect on the basis of conventional economic theory, propagated also by S&N, that we would feel like we are better off. So why do we feel so miserable? The inference is inevitable that absolute income is not the determinant of our life satisfaction but relative incomes are. The fact that income and wealth have become so concentrated in the hands of the 1 % implies that an increasing number of people are feeling relative deprivation. They are not able to keep up with the Joneses and have gone into debt doing so. That is frustrating. The concentration of wealth also brought about the impoverishment of 45 million people. That is another source of misery. So S&N's theories are contradicted by the evidence. Yet, conventional economic theory is not sensitive to real data.
- concentration of power which enables the wealthy to influence the institutions of government to serve their interests. John K. Galbraith coined the concept of countervailing power which is missing from S&N's text. The absence of countervailing power of unions meant that big business could gain the upper hand.
- the significance of imperfect information in the economy for which Joseph Stiglitz and George Akerlof received Nobel Prizes. So the students never learn

one of the basic principles of economics, namely that in the presence of asymmetric information markets are generally inefficient.
- signaling for which Michael Spence received a Nobel Prize and which is an important concept because it indicates how difficult and costly it is to convey information about abilities or quality in the market in a credible way. So one has to invest in credentials, for instance, in order to gain the trust of future employers. The investment in such signals is necessary from the individual's point of view even if they are basically nonproductive and therefore wasteful.
- gender, minorities, urban decay, drug use, incarceration, in other words, all the unseemly aspects of today's urban life in the USA.
- they claim to be scientific and value free but secretly slip in their value judgments, for example, by emphasizing efficiency as a universal good that trumps a just distribution of wealth created by the economy.
- that markets with imperfect information are not efficient at all. And in today's markets asymmetric information is pervasive and makes real markets inefficient.
- that the economy is embedded in a culture which plays an important role in the economy and big business constantly attempts to change this culture in such a way as to be able to increase their profit.
- that almost all of the economy is made up of monopolies and oligopolies. Yet, they focus almost exclusively on perfectly competitive models with perfect information which is a completely negligible part of contemporary economies. As a consequence, their inferences are misleading and are not applicable for the most part to the real existing economy.
- underemployment is neglected completely even though it is an important problem and indicates how much wasted human resources there are in the system.
- that wealth is power and the accumulation of immense wealth on part of corporations provides them immense advantages in bargaining with employees. They exert this power to benefit from the excess supply of labor and depress wages excessively.
- in addition, corporations used their power to exert an inordinate amount of influence on government. S&N do not provide the student with an appreciation of how much this matters in the ability of corporations to exert the pressure on congress and tilt the playing field in favor of big business. Important decisions are made in the interest of the wealthy.
- the concerted attack on the unions and their subsequent demise enabled corporations to take advantage of their power in order to further depress wages.
- their text is very thin on data and evidence and concentrates mainly on theorizing in a veiled ideological manner.
- that median household income has been declining since 1999. And wages, too, have been stagnating for a very long time in spite of the fact that productivity has been increasing.
- that we have paid so little attention to pollution that the very future of the planet is being threatened.

- that aggressive competition for resources and economic advantages in pursuit of self-interest leads to a lot of conflict and stress in the society.
- the need of a sustainable economy so that the next generation can also enjoy this earth as the previous one.

The litany of missing important economic concepts and missing economists could be extended substantially, but it should be clear by now that S&N's text is neither scientific nor does it present economic 'truths' about the real existing economy as they conceitedly claimed in the introduction to their volume. Instead, their text is a tool of indoctrination so that students are socialized into thinking that this is the best imaginable economic system.

They are clandestine supporters of the established power structure, wealth structure, and privilege structure. Moreover, they advocate a dehumanization of economic theory and are complacent about the injustices of the current economic system. They are silent on the fact that our quality of life is under constant pressure and that there has been no progress in our ability to live a stress-free care-free life for generations. Our quality of life and our life satisfaction are simply not commensurate with our productive capacity, because of an obscene distribution of income and because big business has had such a profound effect on the culture and our values. They have captured not only government but also our utility function so that we are made to believe that we can improve our lives through consumption and when that turns out not to be the case we are bewildered, frustrated, even alienated. So we are not more satisfied with our lives than our grandparents were although we are immensely wealthier.

So this is the great irony of our age. We strive to grow the economy; we work more; and in the end, it is all in vein; our life satisfaction remains unchanged or even declines; our unprecedented wealth does not lead to a dignified life for most of the population. This is nothing less than an immense inconsistency with the predictions of mainstream economic theory. Yet, mainstream economic theory lives on in spite of all these inconsistencies with the real world. It seems basically immune to empirical evidence.

The purpose of this book is to demonstrate the poverty of their arguments and in the process sketch the outlines of a progressive agenda. We need a humanistic economics, one which puts flesh and blood human beings in its focus and not a caricature that exists only in the fantasy of economists. We need a capitalism that puts people first and not profit margins, which enables all to live a dignified life and does not relegate a goodly portion of the society into an unbearably inferior status. However, there can be no doubt that such a *Capitalism with a Human Face* cannot be contemplated as long as the next generation learns its economics from such textbooks.

MIX
Papier aus verantwortungsvollen Quellen
Paper from responsible sources
FSC® C105338

If you have any concerns about our products,
you can contact us on
ProductSafety@springernature.com

In case Publisher is established outside the EU,
the EU authorized representative is:
Springer Nature Customer Service Center GmbH
Europaplatz 3, 69115 Heidelberg, Germany

Printed by Libri Plureos GmbH
in Hamburg, Germany